The Underground Railroad

written by
Joe Dunn

illustrated by
Rod Espinosa

magic
wagon

visit us at
www.abdopublishing.com

Published by Magic Wagon, a division of the ABDO Publishing Group, 8000 West 78th Street, Edina, Minnesota 55439. Copyright © 2008 by Abdo Consulting Group, Inc. International copyrights reserved in all countries. All rights reserved. No part of this book may be reproduced in any form without written permission from the publisher. Graphic Planet™ is a trademark and logo of Magic Wagon.

Printed in the United States.

Written by Joe Dunn
Illustrated by Rod Espinosa
Colored and lettered by Rod Espinosa
Edited by Stephanie Hedlund
Interior layout and design by Antarctic Press
Cover art by Rod Espinosa
Cover design by Neil Klinepier

Library of Congress Cataloging-in-Publication Data

Dunn, Joeming W.
   Underground Railroad / written by Joe Dunn and illustrated by Rod Espinosa.
   p. cm. -- (Graphic history)
   Includes index.
   ISBN 978-1-60270-080-2
   1. Underground Railroad--Juvenile literature. 2. Fugitive slaves--United States--History--19th century--Juvenile literature. 3. Antislavery movements--United States--History--19th century--Juvenile literature. I. Title.

E450.E85 2007
 973.7'115--dc22
                               2007012067

TABLE of CONTENTS

This is Harriet Tubman. She helped free plenty of slaves. She was part of the Underground Railroad.

What is the Underground Railroad, and why is it important today?

To find the answers, we must go back to the early 1800s, a time when slavery in the United States was still practiced...

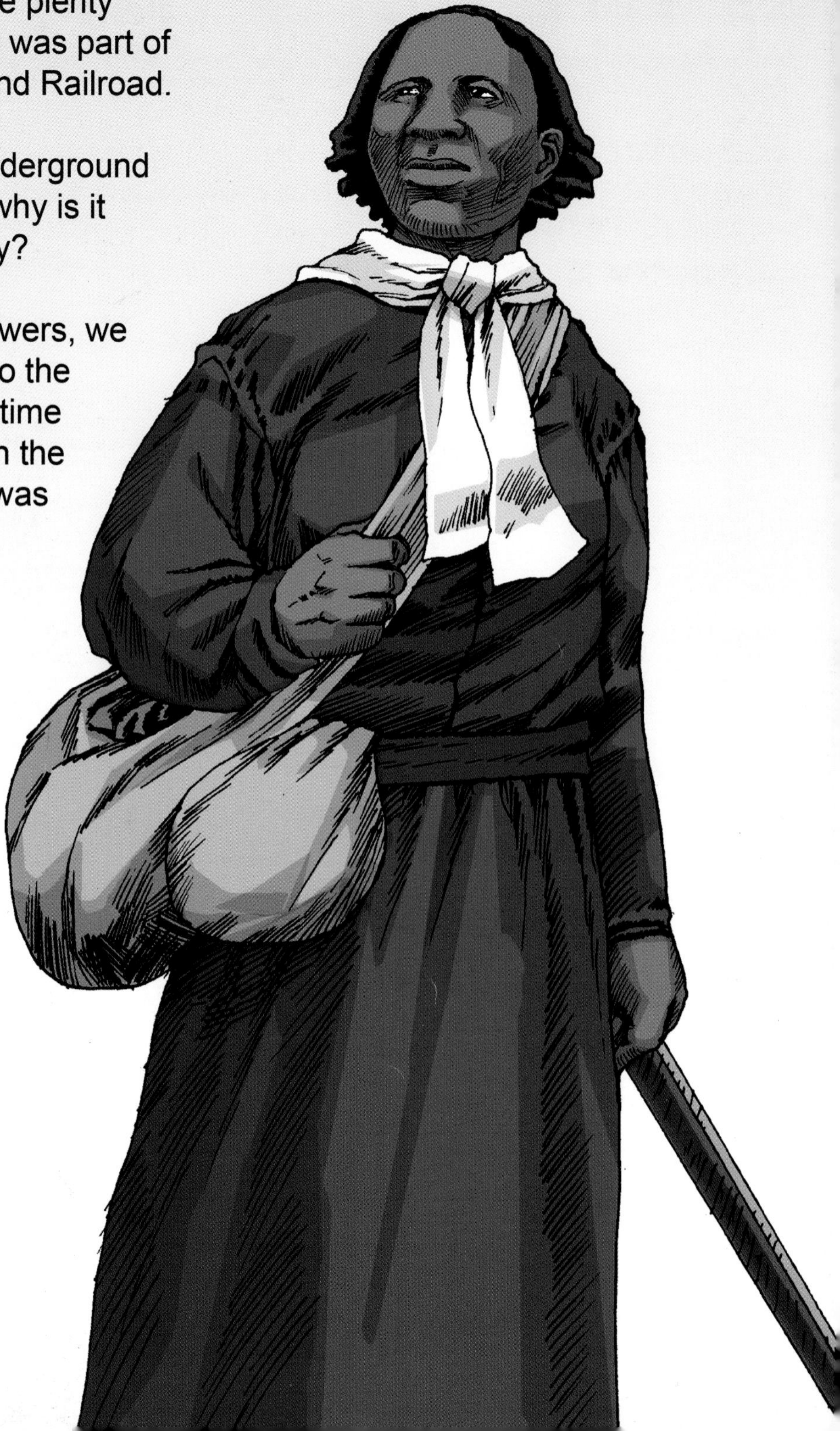

Chapter 1 Freedom's Trail

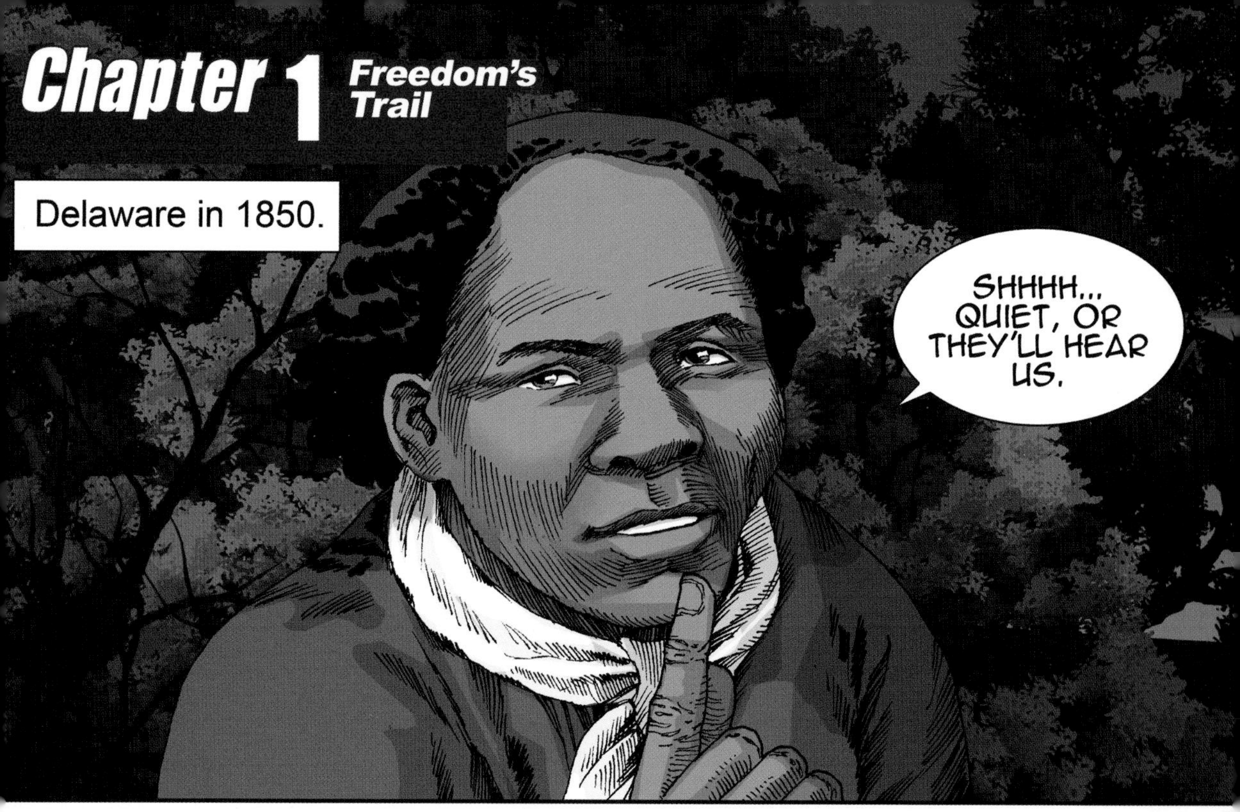
Delaware in 1850.
SHHHH... QUIET, OR THEY'LL HEAR US.

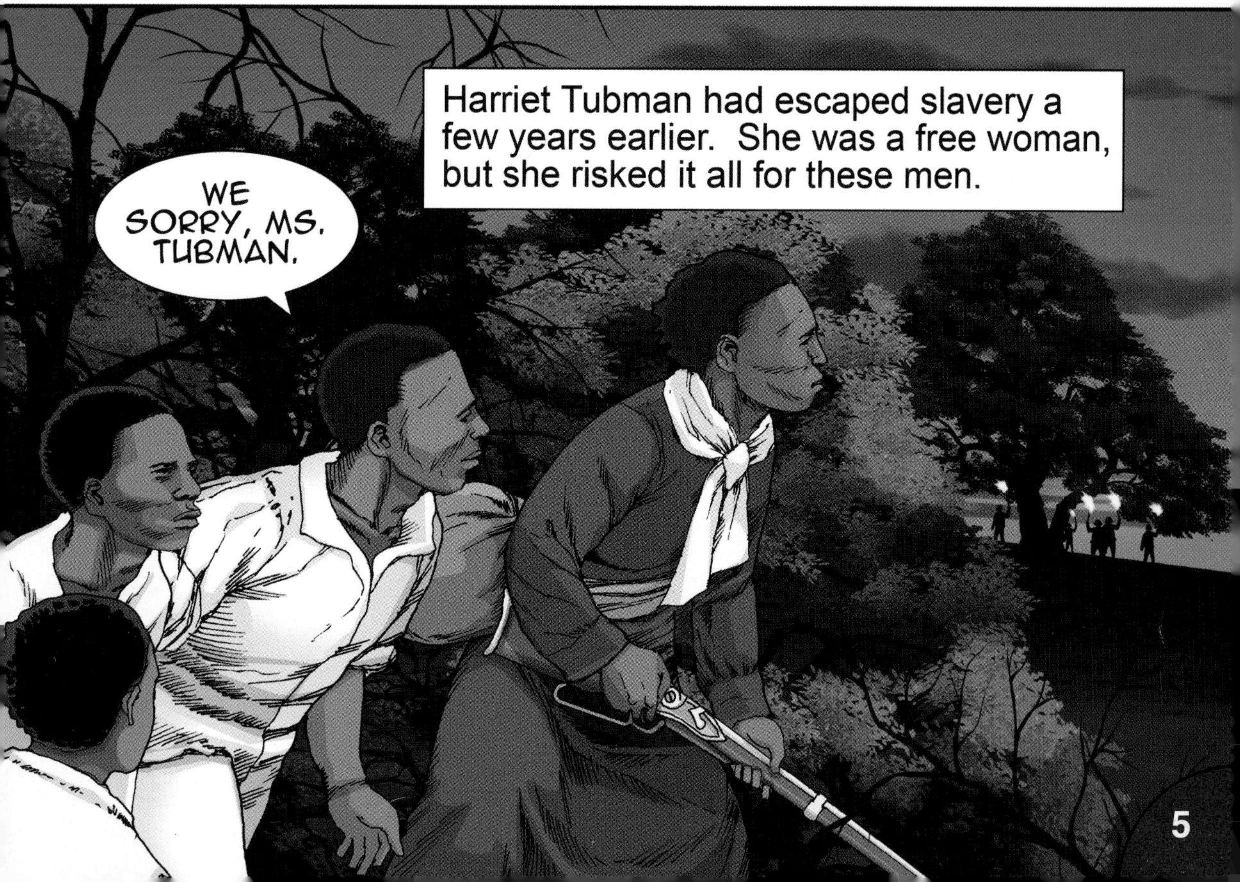
Harriet Tubman had escaped slavery a few years earlier. She was a free woman, but she risked it all for these men.
WE SORRY, MS. TUBMAN.

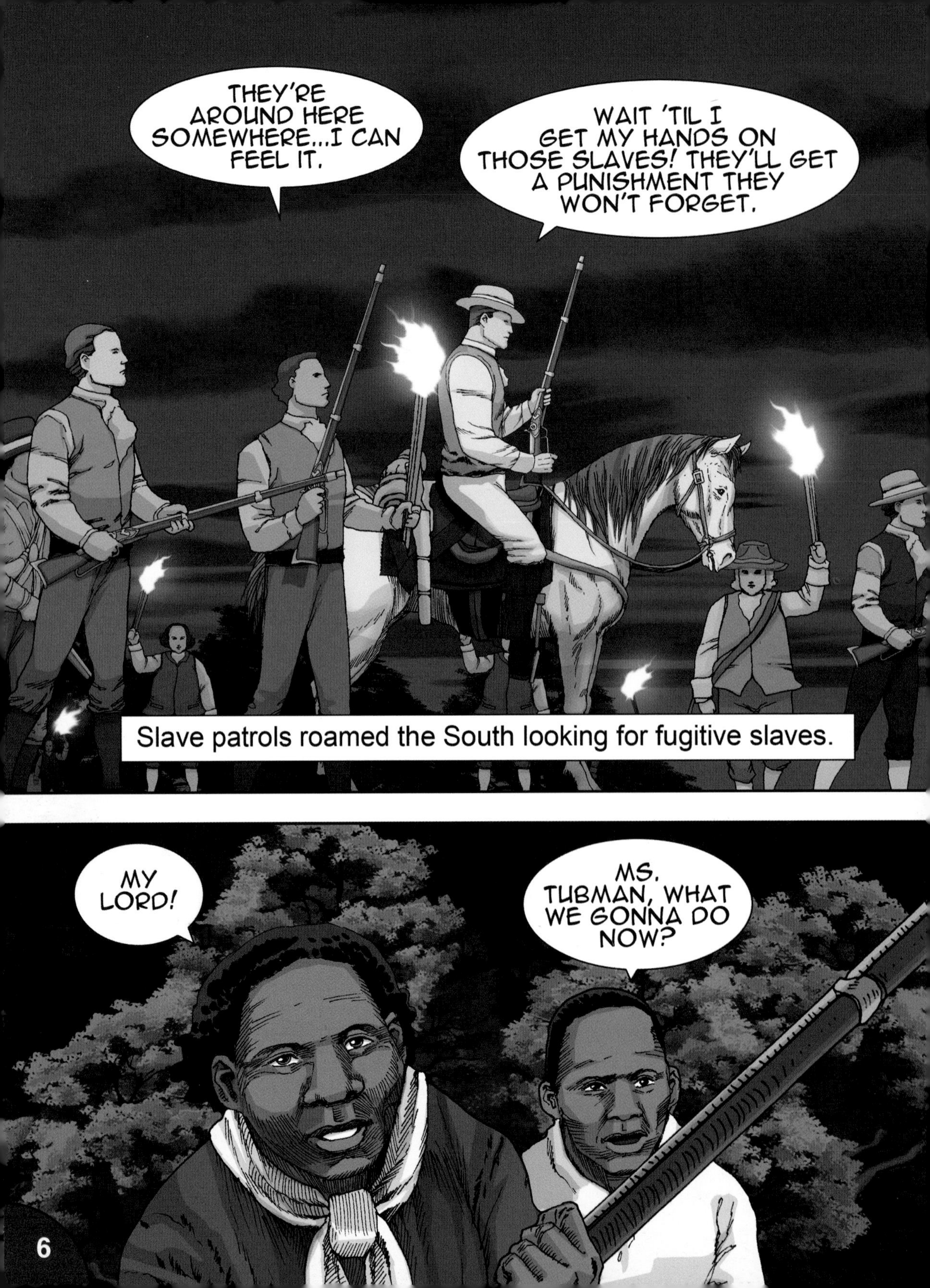
THEY'RE AROUND HERE SOMEWHERE...I CAN FEEL IT.
WAIT 'TIL I GET MY HANDS ON THOSE SLAVES! THEY'LL GET A PUNISHMENT THEY WON'T FORGET.
Slave patrols roamed the South looking for fugitive slaves.
MY LORD!
MS. TUBMAN, WHAT WE GONNA DO NOW?

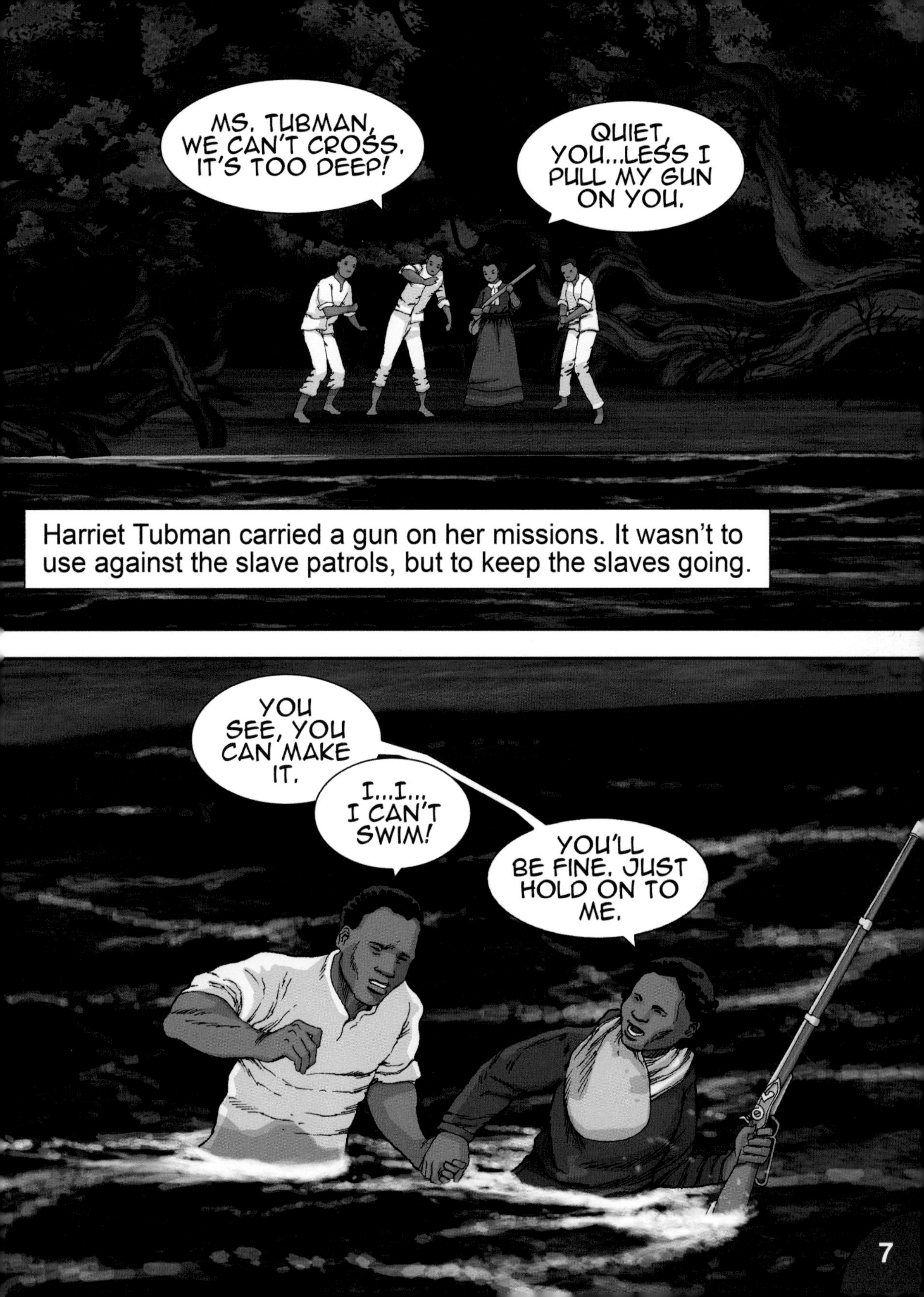
MS. TUBMAN, WE CAN'T CROSS. IT'S TOO DEEP!
QUIET, YOU...LESS I PULL MY GUN ON YOU.
Harriet Tubman carried a gun on her missions. It wasn't to use against the slave patrols, but to keep the slaves going.
YOU SEE, YOU CAN MAKE IT.
I...I... I CAN'T SWIM!
YOU'LL BE FINE. JUST HOLD ON TO ME.

n had gone through worse. This was nothing
ed to some of the hardships she had endured.

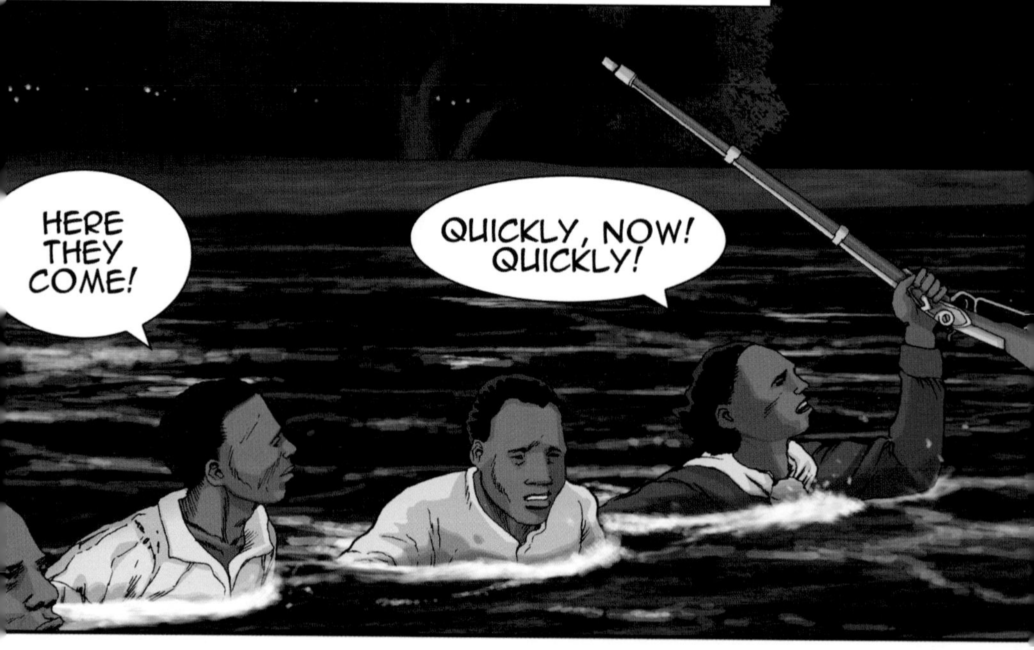
HERE THEY COME!
QUICKLY, NOW! QUICKLY!

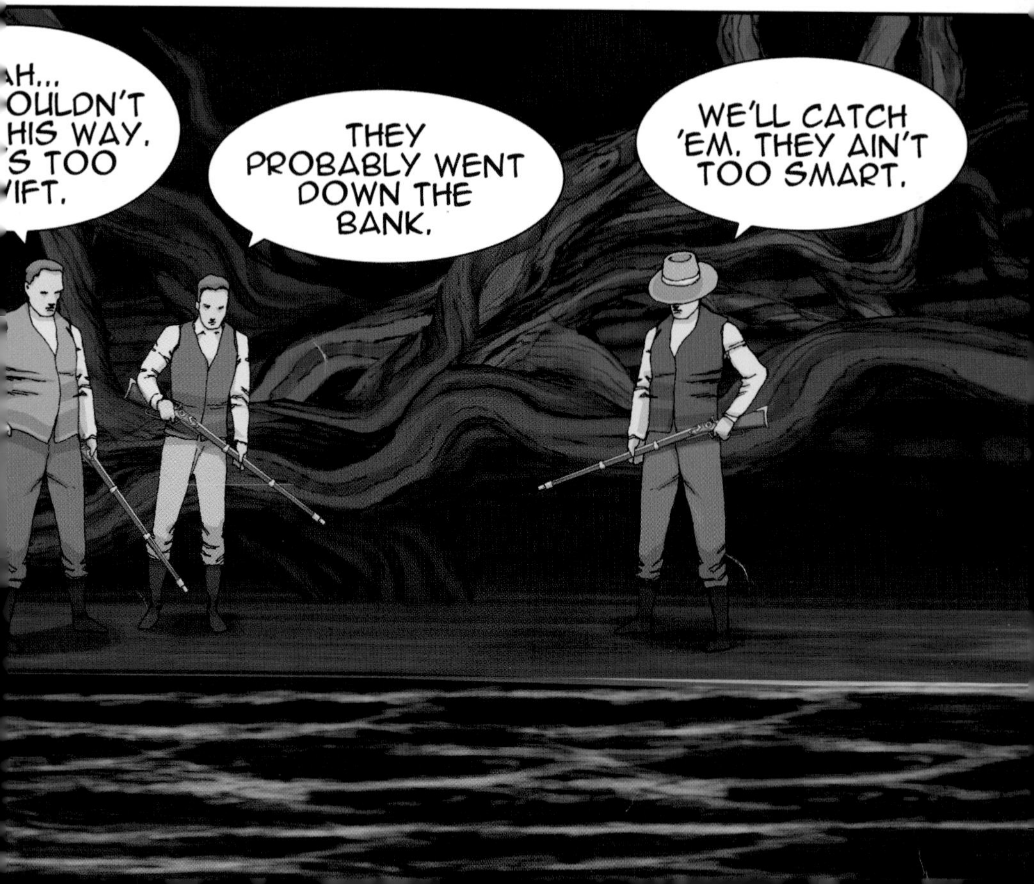
AH... OULDN'T HIS WAY. S TOO IFT.
THEY PROBABLY WENT DOWN THE BANK.
WE'LL CATCH 'EM. THEY AIN'T TOO SMART.

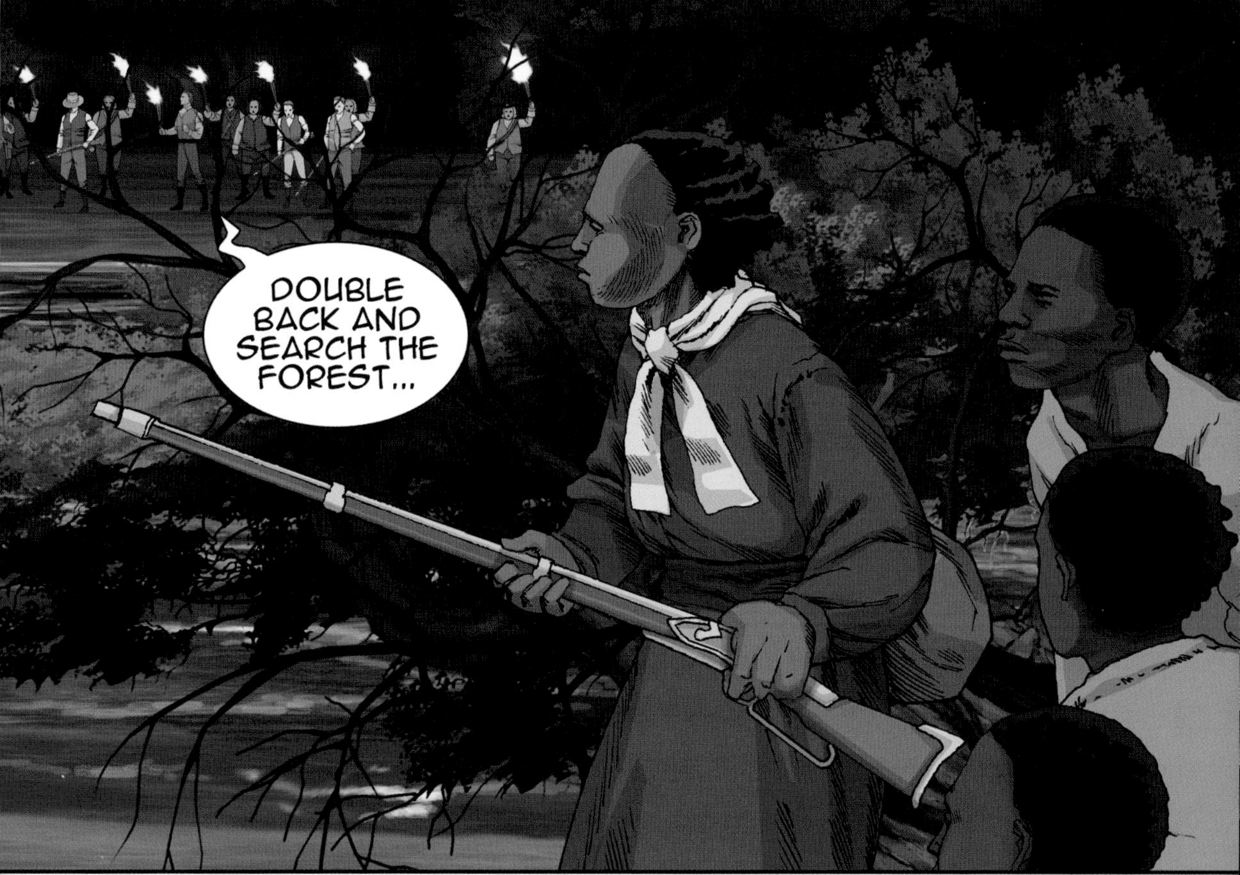
DOUBLE BACK AND SEARCH THE FOREST...

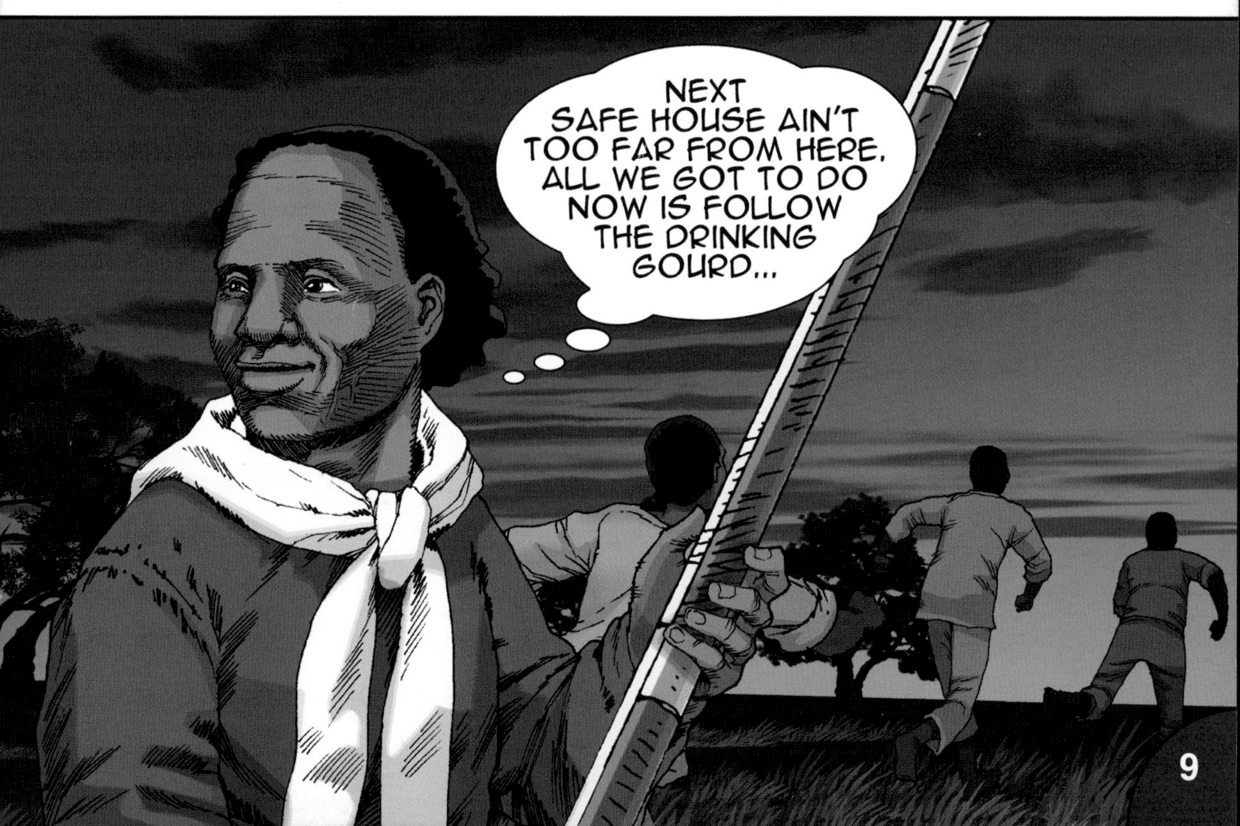
NEXT SAFE HOUSE AIN'T TOO FAR FROM HERE. ALL WE GOT TO DO NOW IS FOLLOW THE DRINKING GOURD...

Chapter 2 Slaves in the New World

Slavery can be traced to the establishment of Jamestown in 1619. Back then, many people could not afford to travel to the New World.

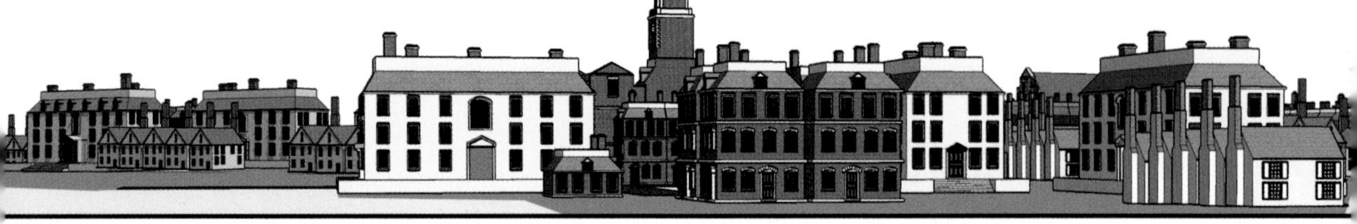

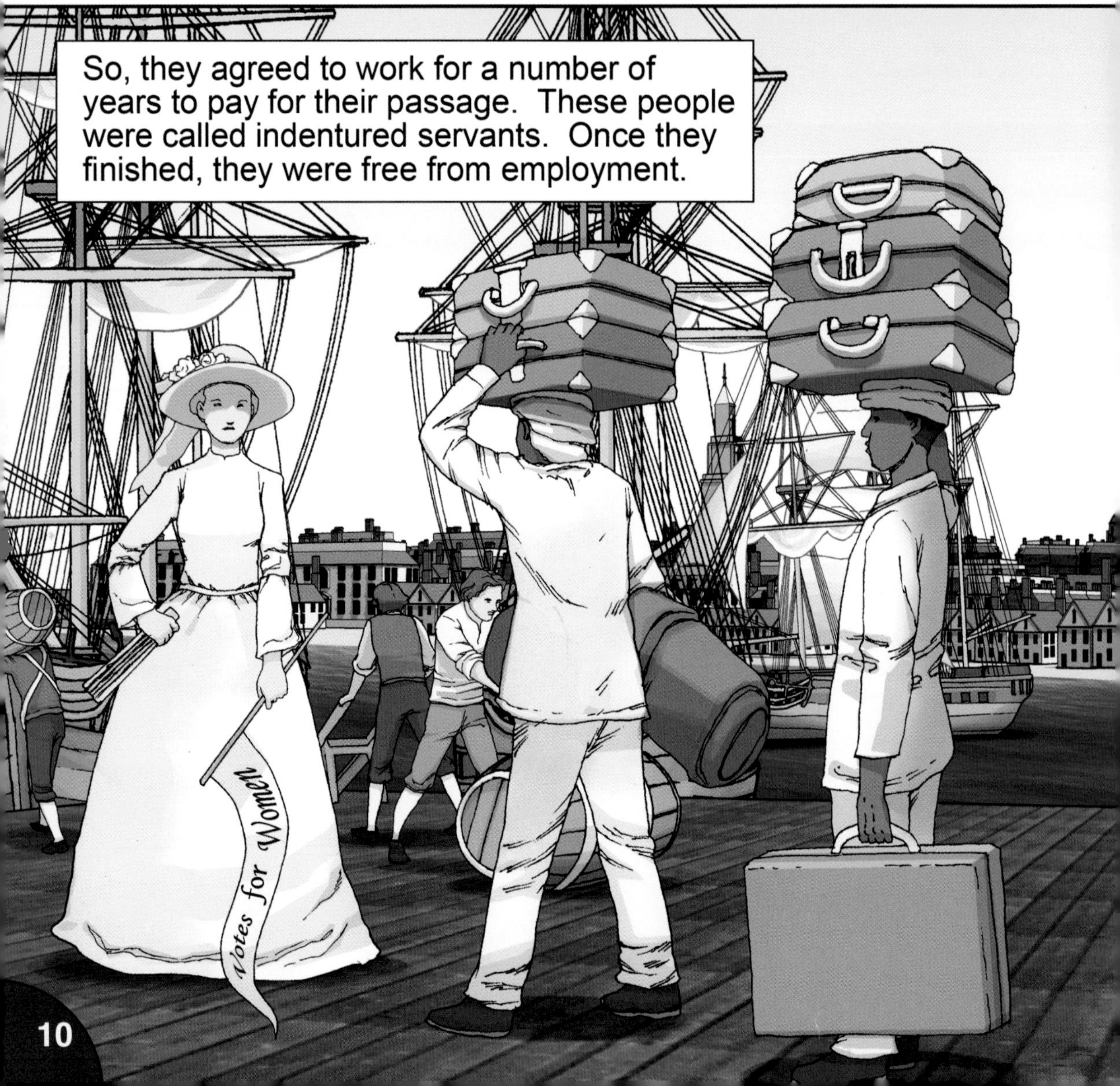
So, they agreed to work for a number of years to pay for their passage. These people were called indentured servants. Once they finished, they were free from employment.
Votes for Women

Tobacco was one of the main crops of the time. It took time, labor, and large tracts of land to produce. To meet this demand, the plantation owners needed more slaves.

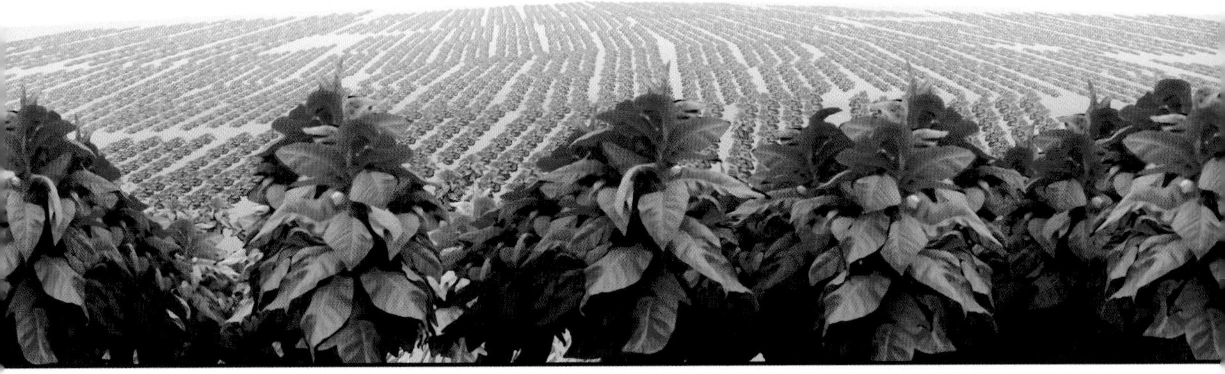

In the mid-1600s, the indentured servants had to work for many more years to pay their debts. Sometimes they would serve for life. Many others did not have the option of freedom.

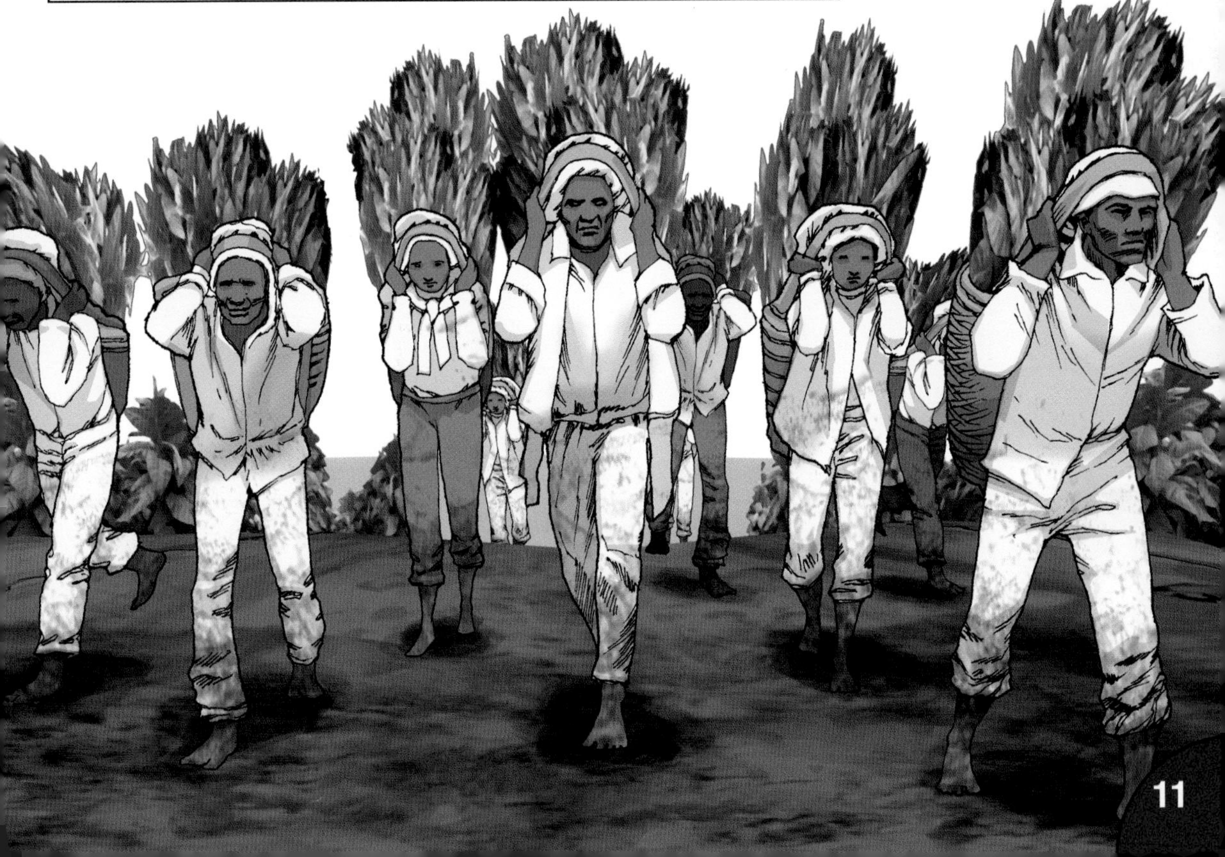

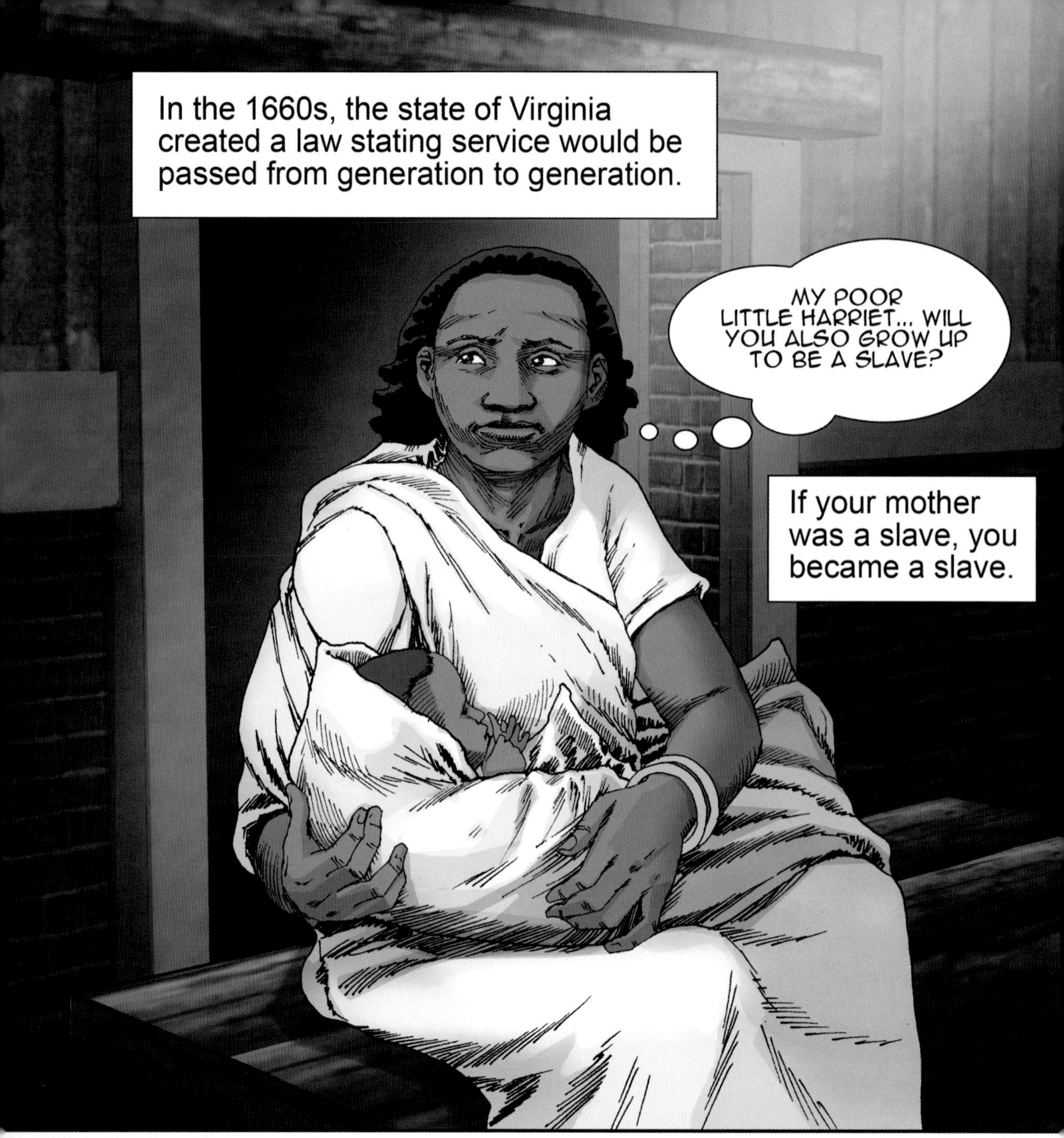
In the 1660s, the state of Virginia created a law stating service would be passed from generation to generation.
MY POOR LITTLE HARRIET... WILL YOU ALSO GROW UP TO BE A SLAVE?
If your mother was a slave, you became a slave.

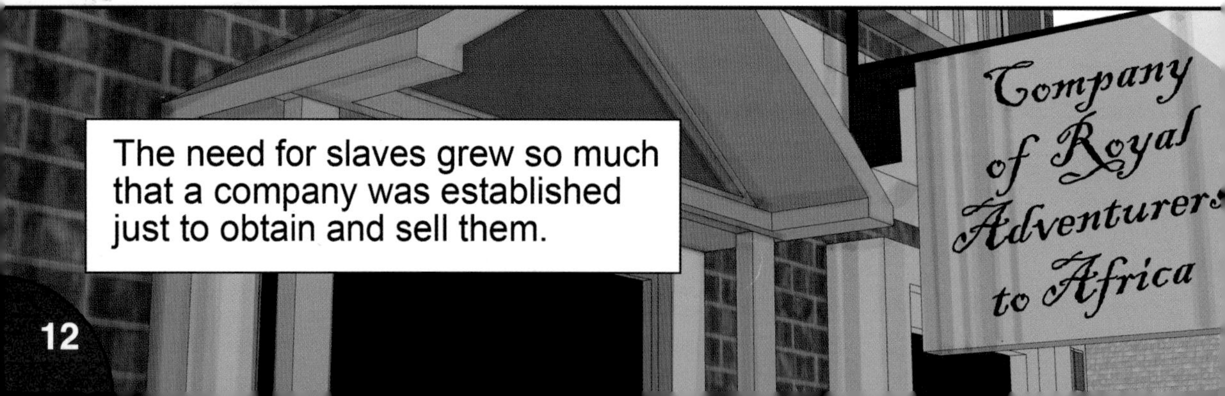
The need for slaves grew so much that a company was established just to obtain and sell them.
Company of Royal Adventurers to Africa

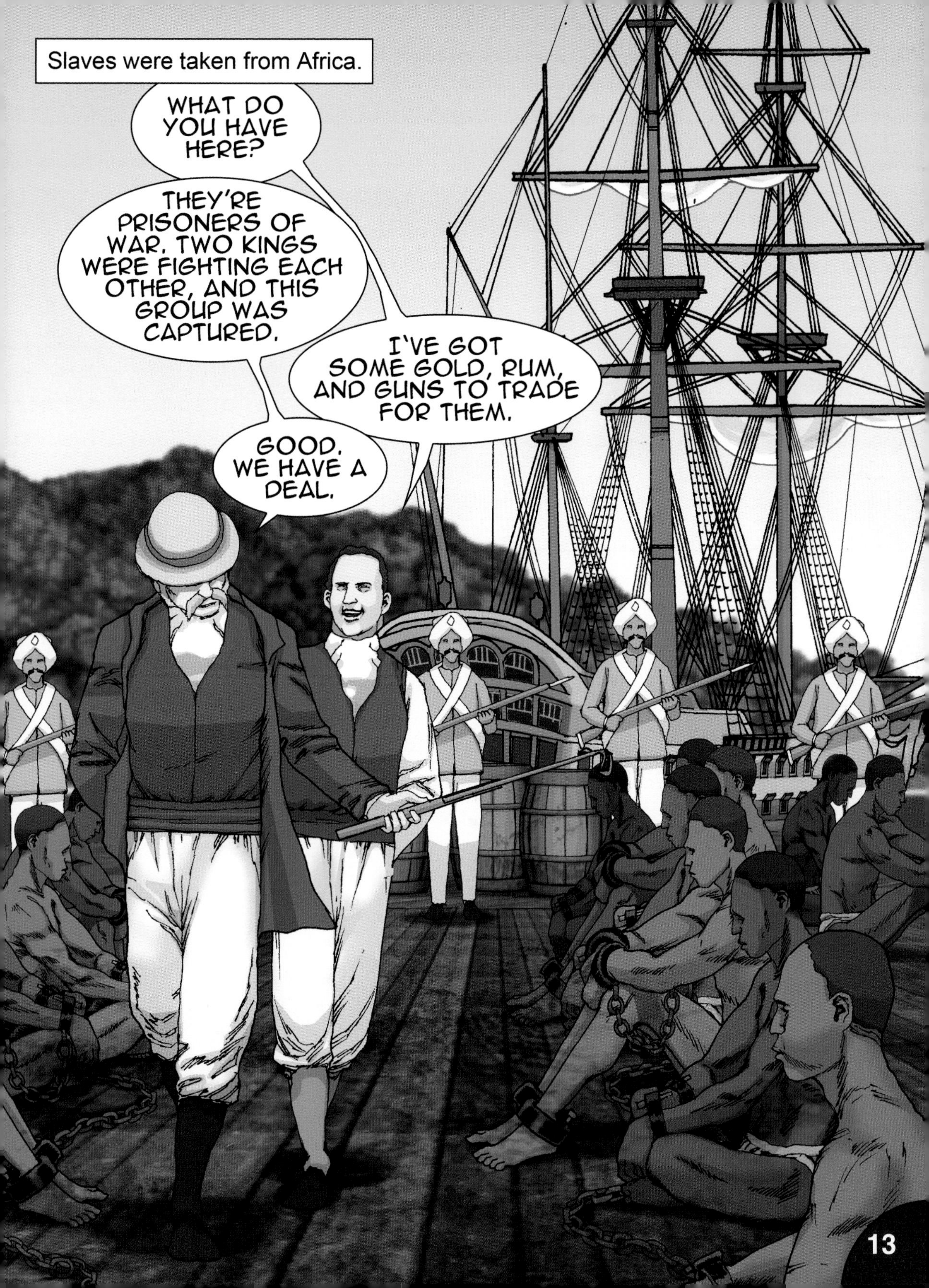
Slaves were taken from Africa.
WHAT DO YOU HAVE HERE?
THEY'RE PRISONERS OF WAR. TWO KINGS WERE FIGHTING EACH OTHER, AND THIS GROUP WAS CAPTURED.
I'VE GOT SOME GOLD, RUM, AND GUNS TO TRADE FOR THEM.
GOOD. WE HAVE A DEAL.

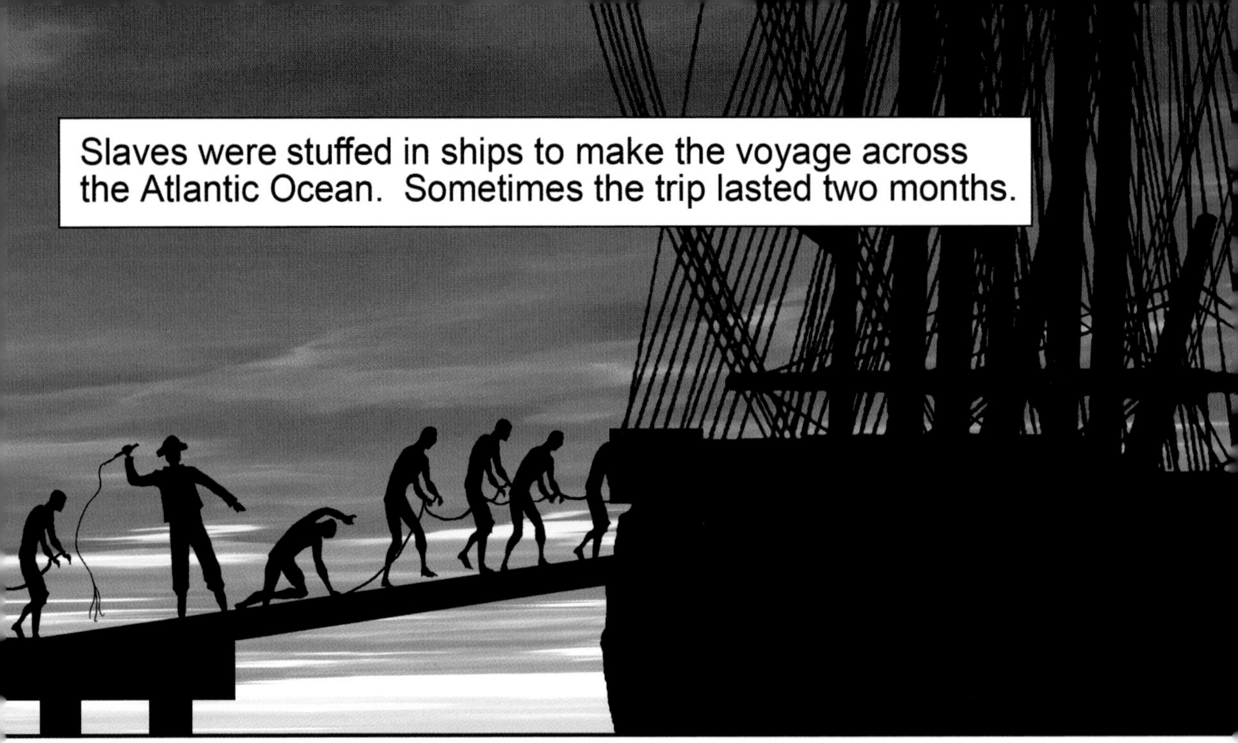
Slaves were stuffed in ships to make the voyage across the Atlantic Ocean. Sometimes the trip lasted two months.

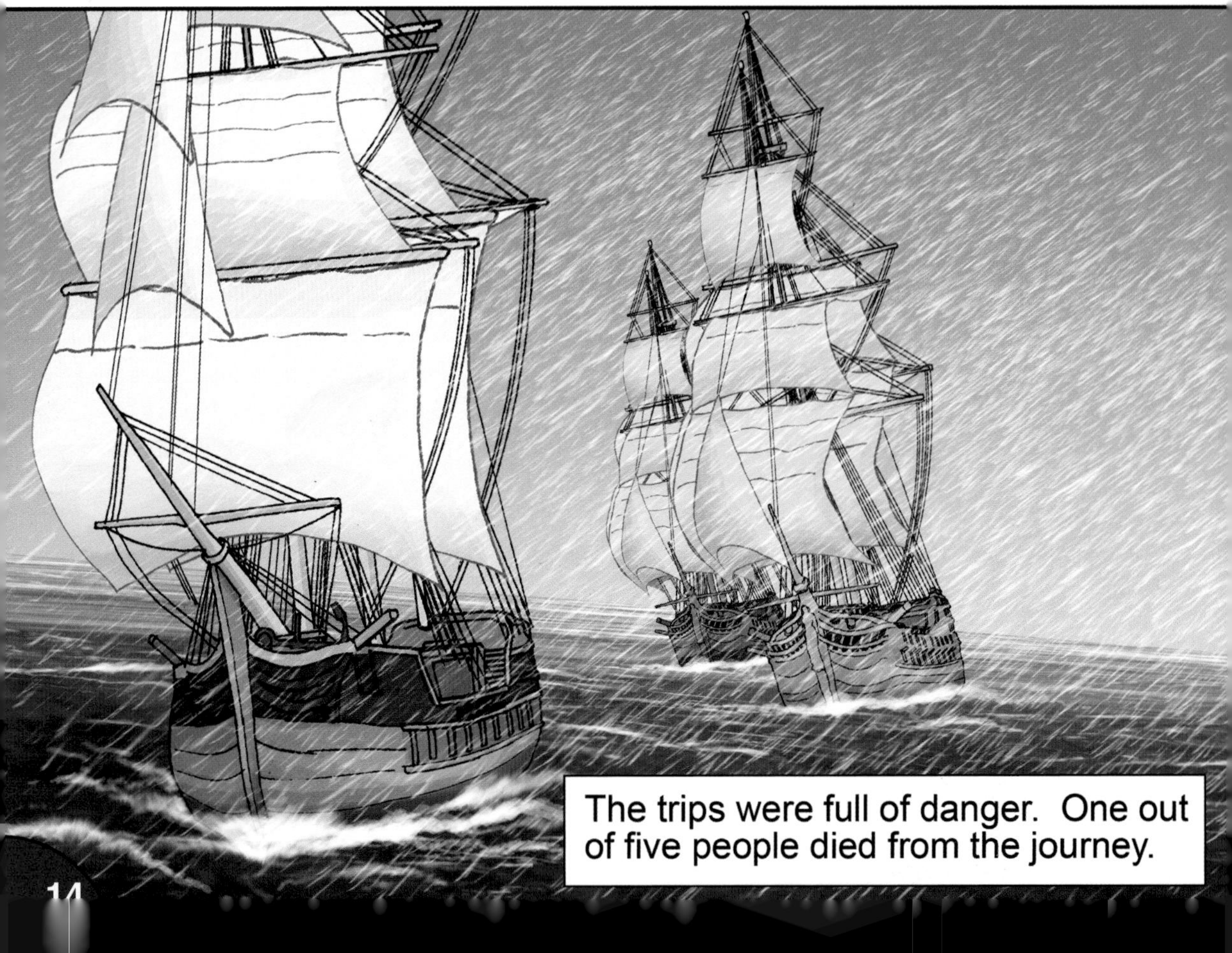
The trips were full of danger. One out of five people died from the journey.

Chapter 3 Slave Life

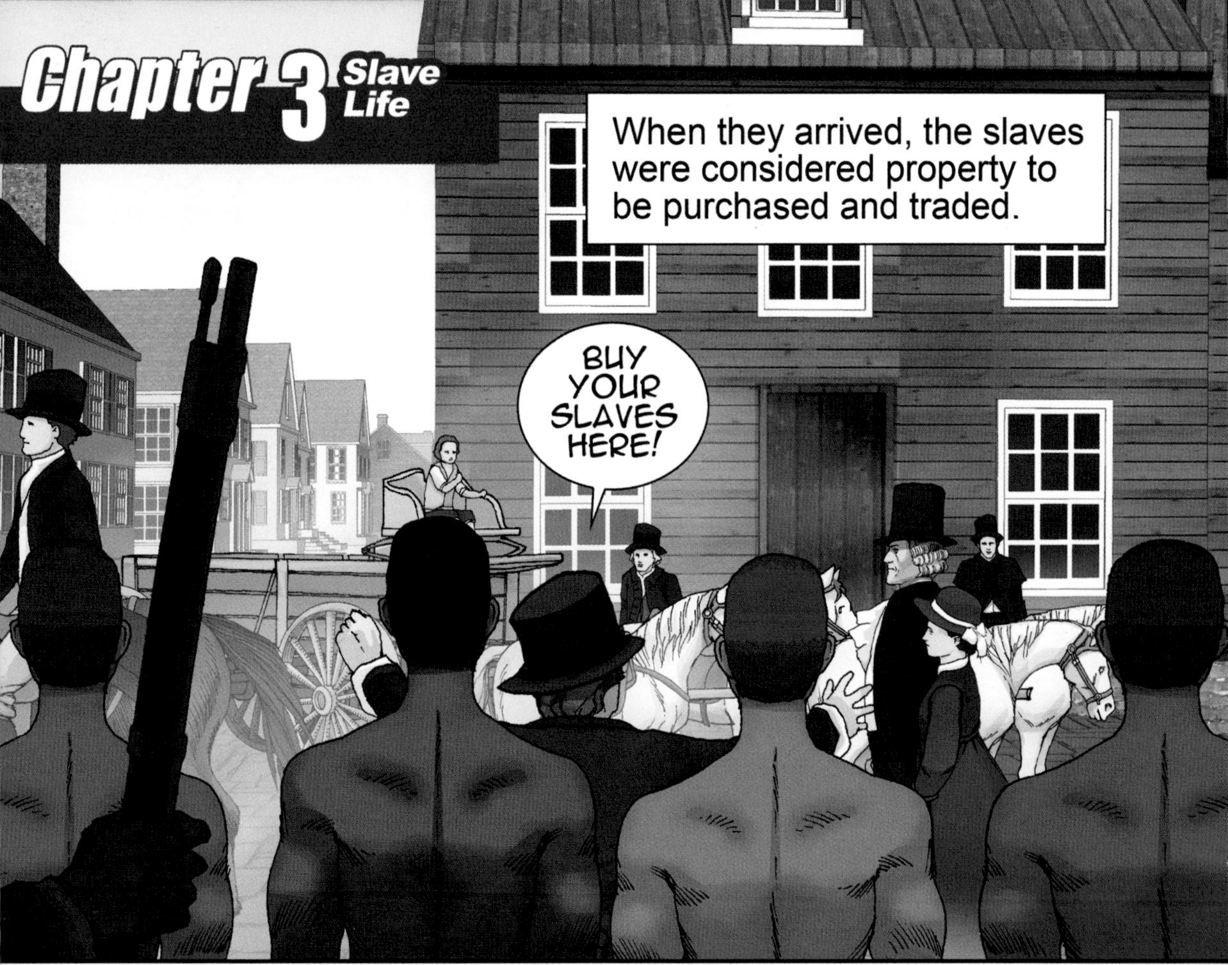
When they arrived, the slaves were considered property to be purchased and traded.
BUY YOUR SLAVES HERE!

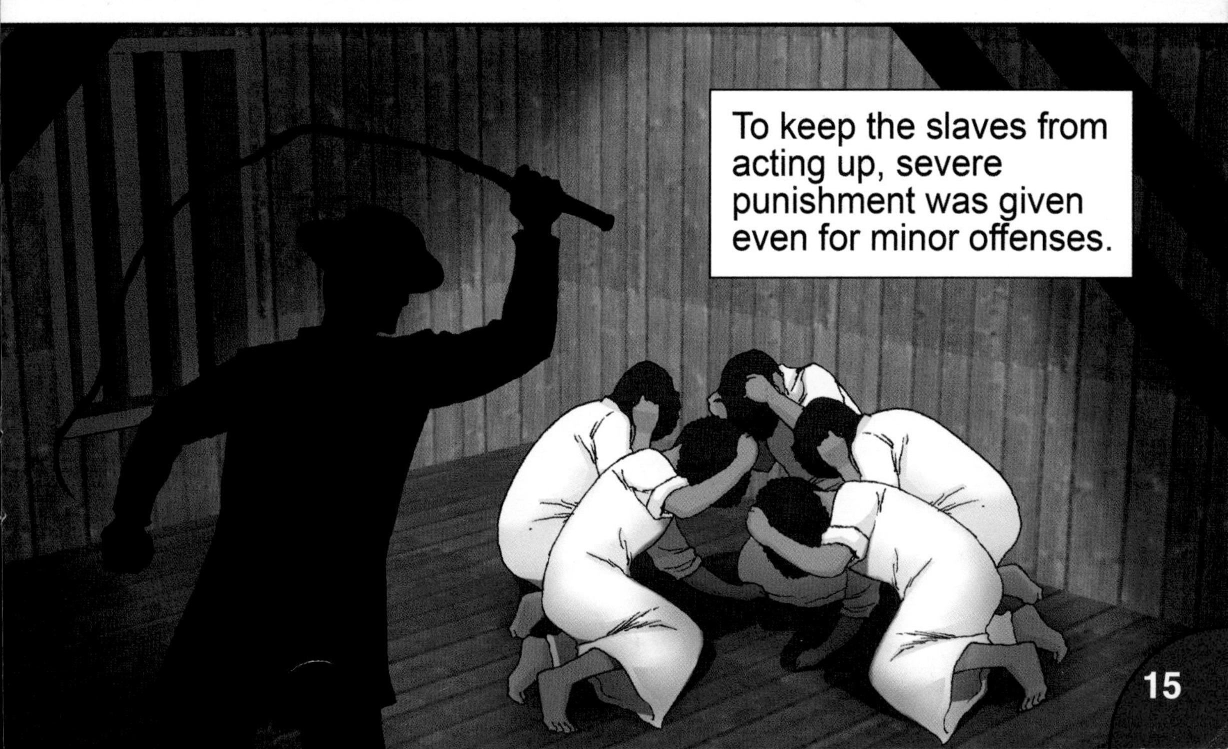
To keep the slaves from acting up, severe punishment was given even for minor offenses.

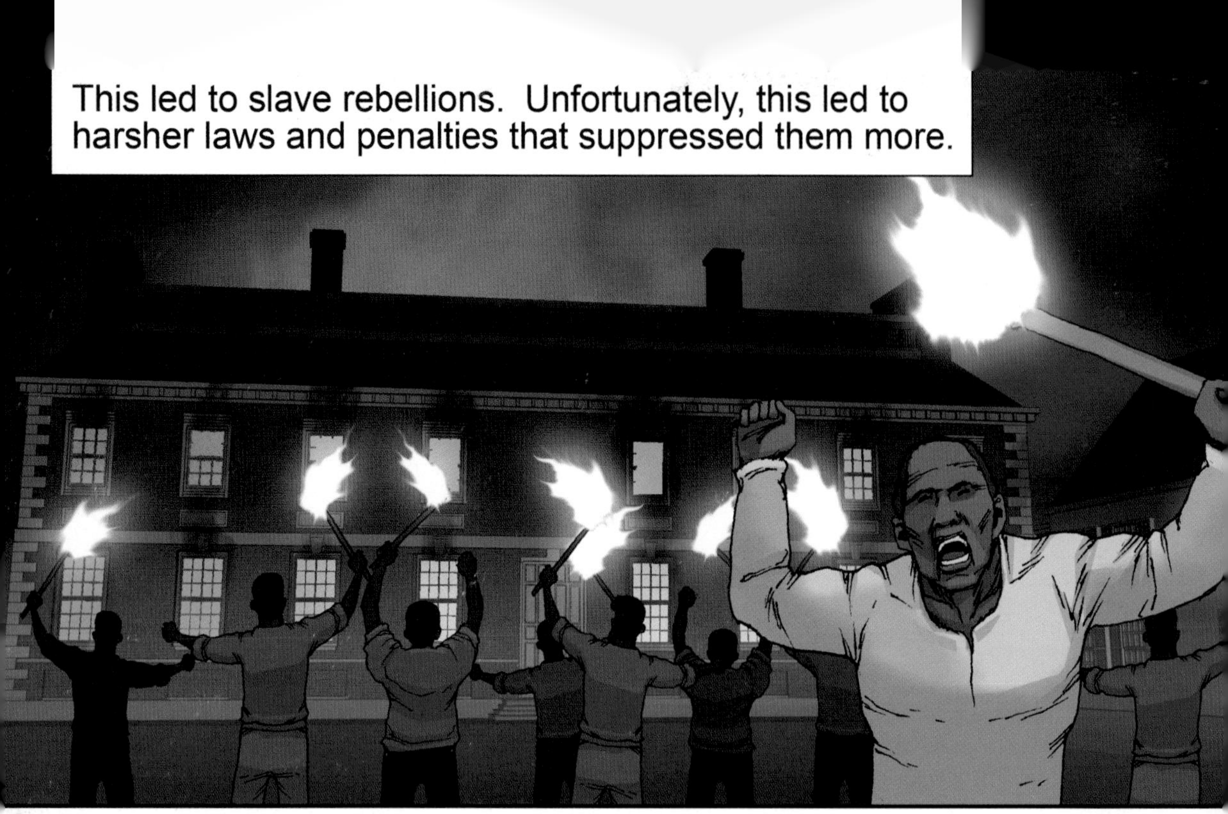
This led to slave rebellions. Unfortunately, this led to harsher laws and penalties that suppressed them more.

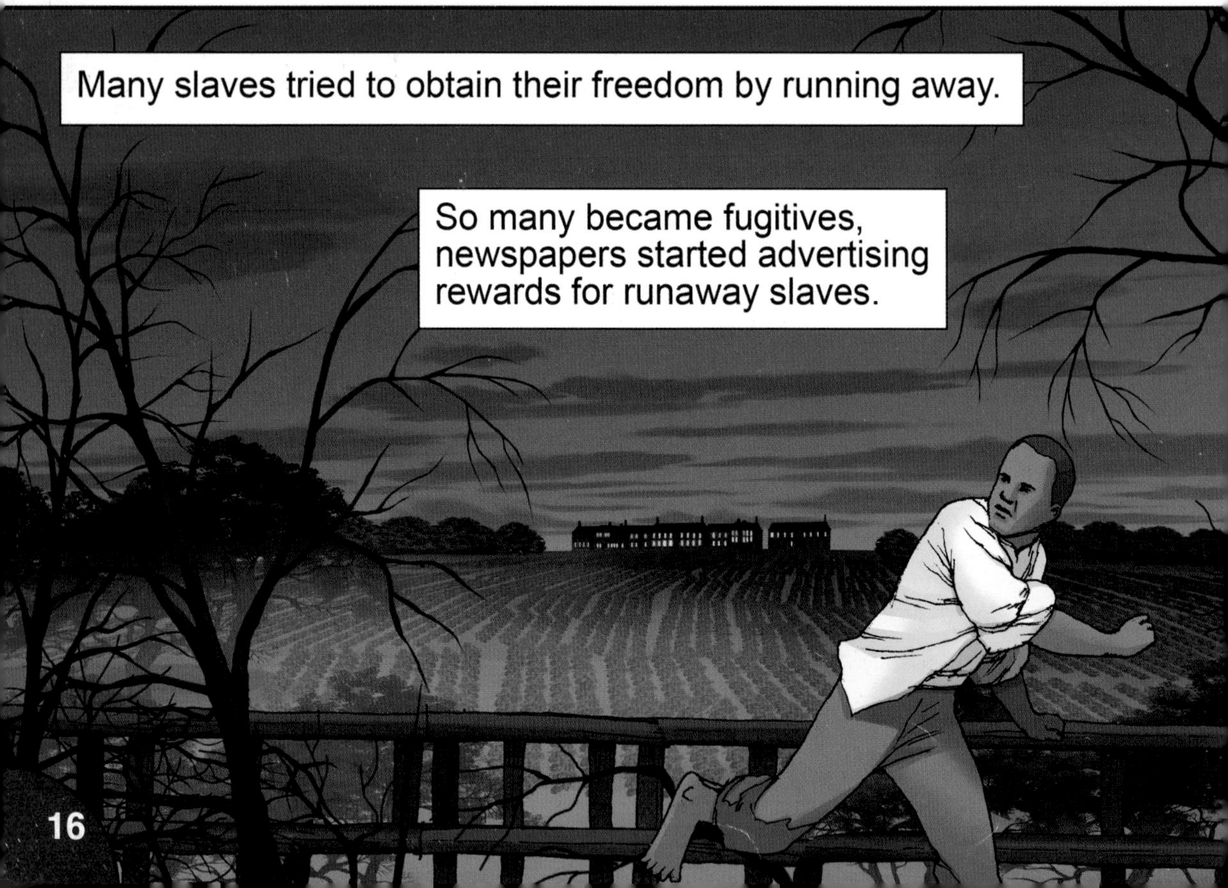
Many slaves tried to obtain their freedom by running away.
So many became fugitives, newspapers started advertising rewards for runaway slaves.

Chapter 4 Rise of the Abolitionists

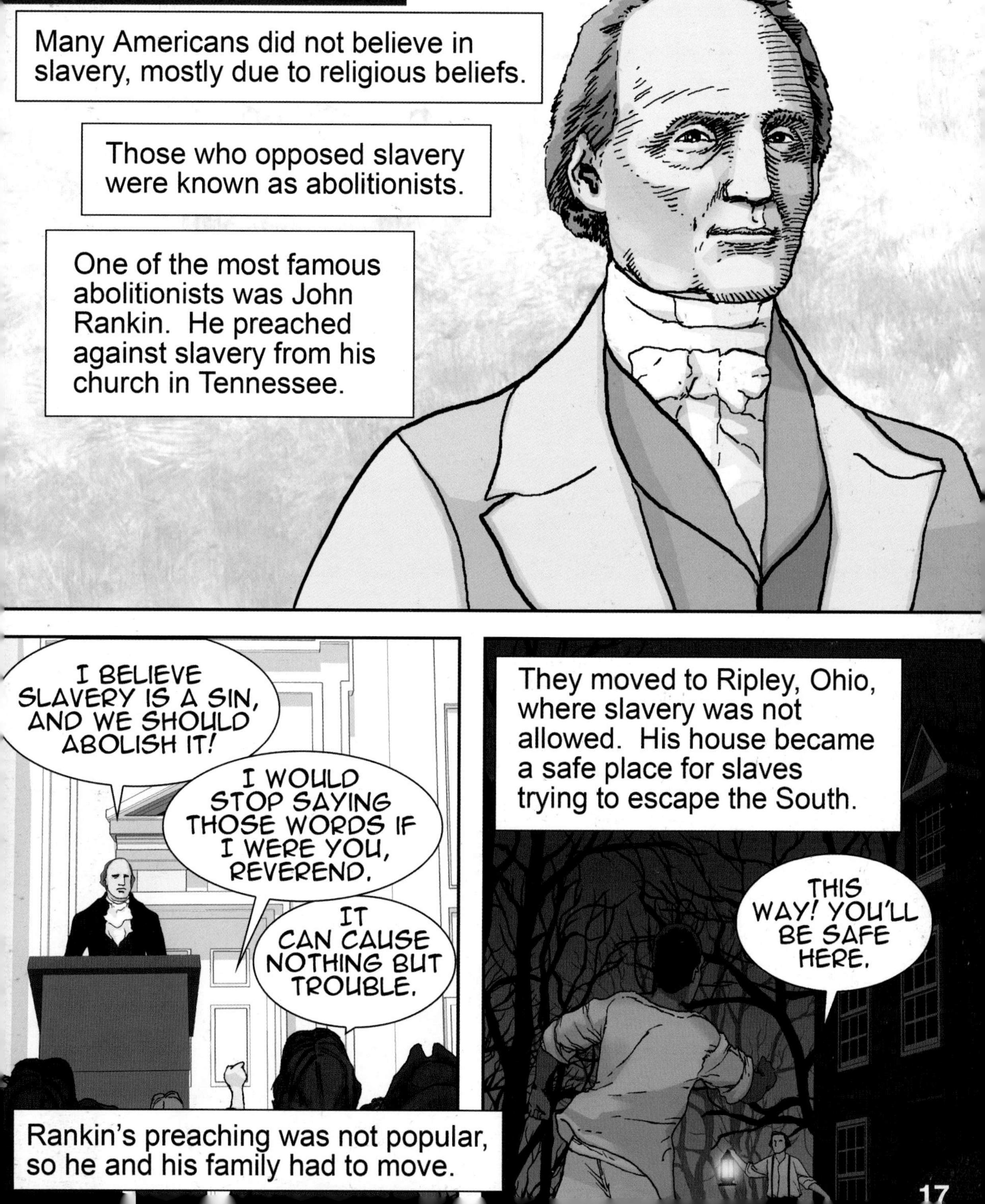
Many Americans did not believe in slavery, mostly due to religious beliefs.
Those who opposed slavery were known as abolitionists.
One of the most famous abolitionists was John Rankin. He preached against slavery from his church in Tennessee.
I BELIEVE SLAVERY IS A SIN, AND WE SHOULD ABOLISH IT!
I WOULD STOP SAYING THOSE WORDS IF I WERE YOU, REVEREND.
IT CAN CAUSE NOTHING BUT TROUBLE.
Rankin's preaching was not popular, so he and his family had to move.
They moved to Ripley, Ohio, where slavery was not allowed. His house became a safe place for slaves trying to escape the South.
THIS WAY! YOU'LL BE SAFE HERE.

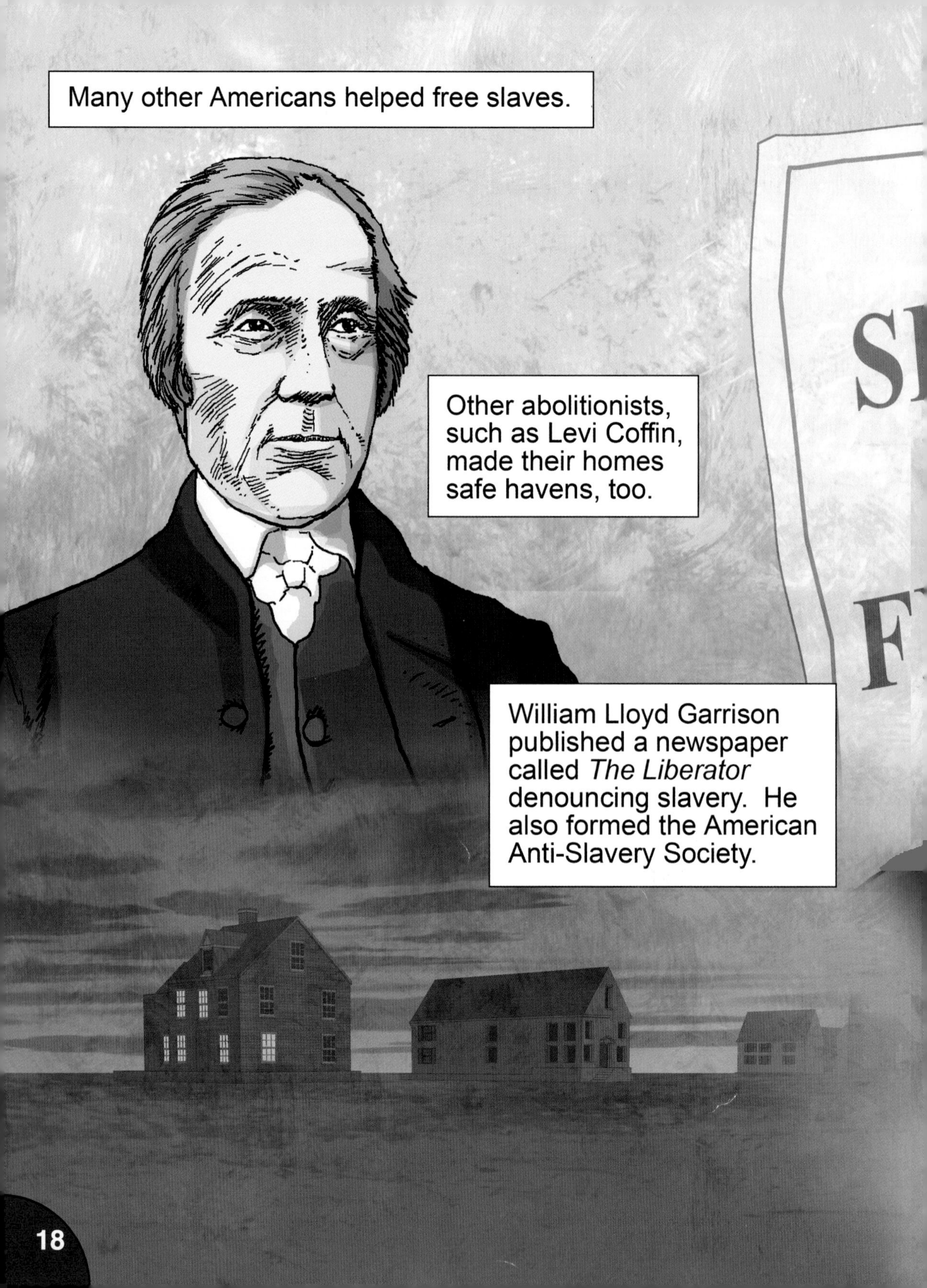

Many other Americans helped free slaves.
Other abolitionists, such as Levi Coffin, made their homes safe havens, too.
William Lloyd Garrison published a newspaper called *The Liberator* denouncing slavery. He also formed the American Anti-Slavery Society.

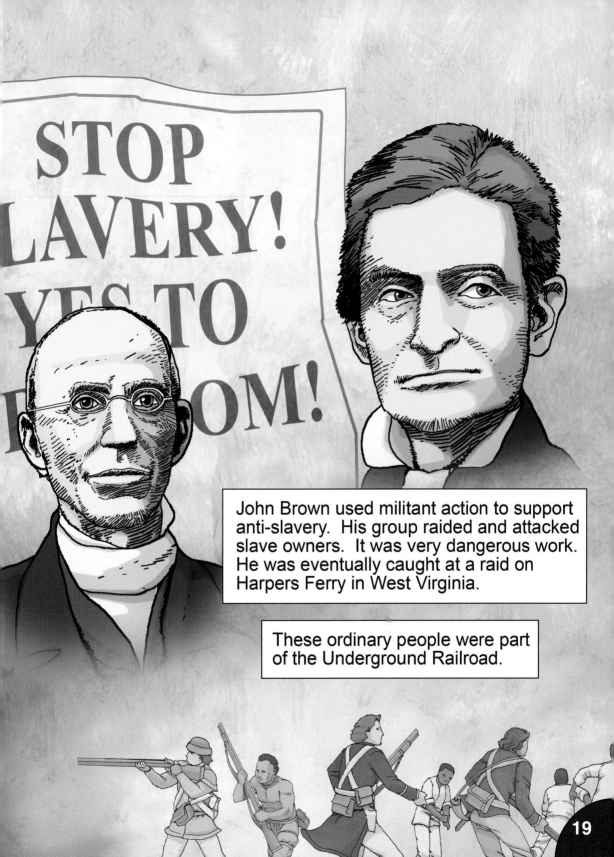

STOP
LAVERY!
YES TO
OM!

John Brown used militant action to support anti-slavery. His group raided and attacked slave owners. It was very dangerous work. He was eventually caught at a raid on Harpers Ferry in West Virginia.

These ordinary people were part of the Underground Railroad.

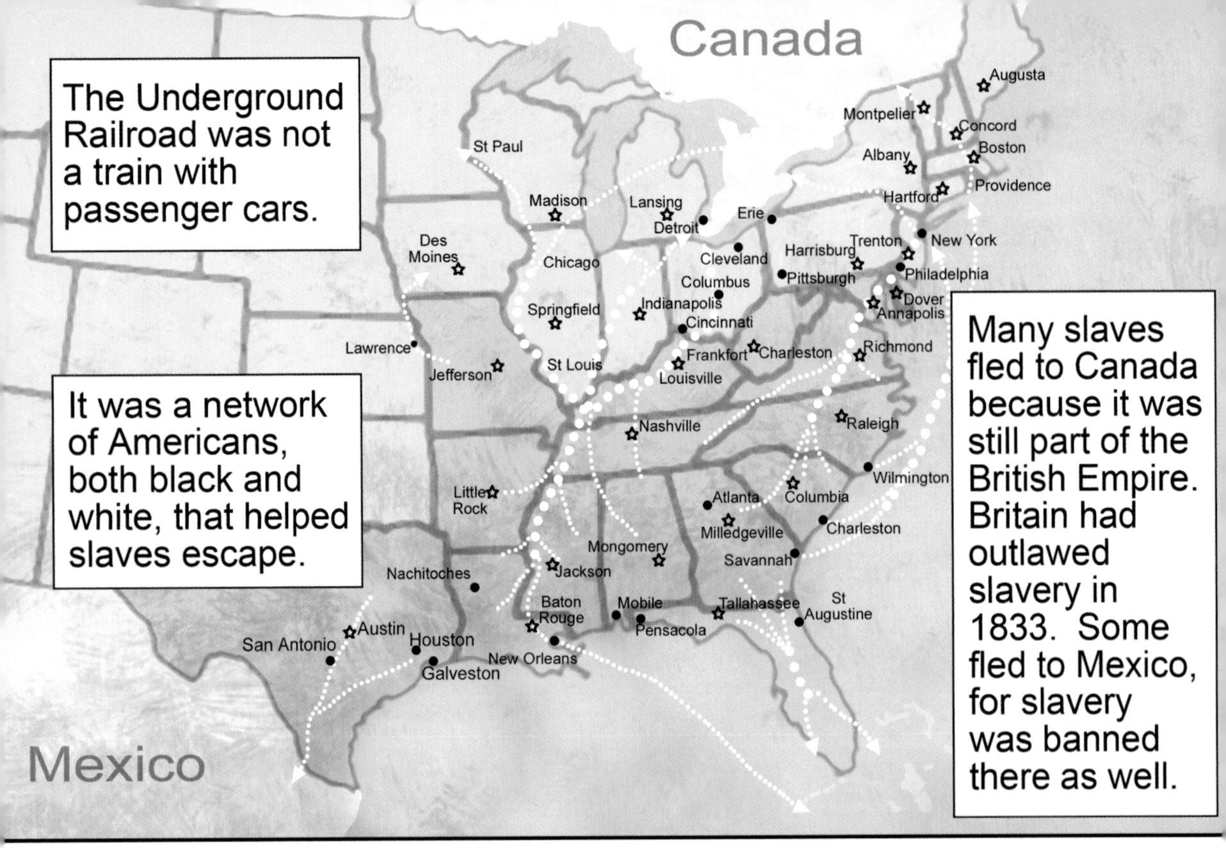
The Underground Railroad was not a train with passenger cars.
It was a network of Americans, both black and white, that helped slaves escape.
Many slaves fled to Canada because it was still part of the British Empire. Britain had outlawed slavery in 1833. Some fled to Mexico, for slavery was banned there as well.
Canada
Mexico
Augusta
Montpelier
Concord
Boston
Albany
Providence
Hartford
St Paul
Madison
Lansing
Detroit
Erie
New York
Trenton
Harrisburg
Des Moines
Chicago
Cleveland
Pittsburgh
Philadelphia
Columbus
Dover
Annapolis
Springfield
Indianapolis
Cincinnati
Lawrence
Richmond
Frankfort
Charleston
Jefferson
St Louis
Louisville
Raleigh
Nashville
Wilmington
Little Rock
Atlanta
Columbia
Milledgeville
Charleston
Mongomery
Savannah
Jackson
Nachitoches
Baton Rouge
Mobile
Tallahassee
St Augustine
Pensacola
Austin
Houston
San Antonio
New Orleans
Galveston

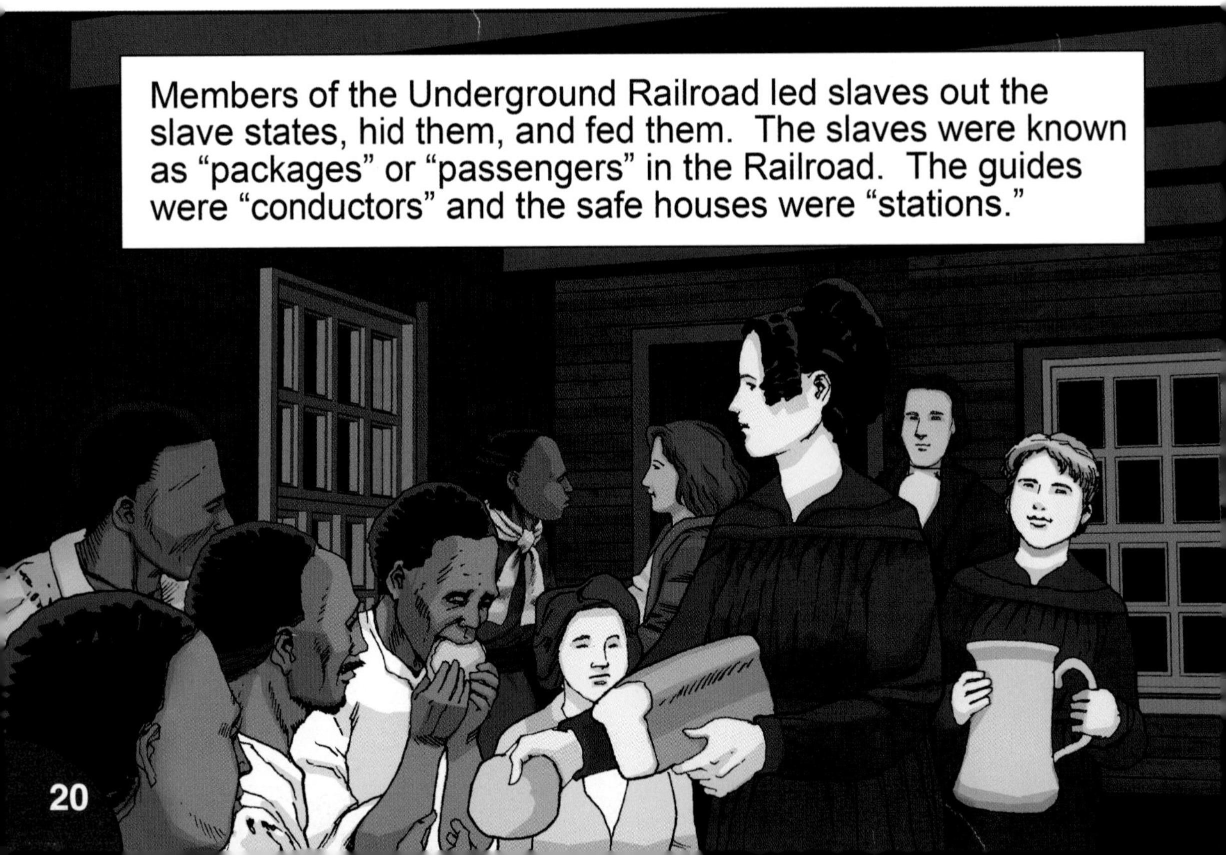
Members of the Underground Railroad led slaves out the slave states, hid them, and fed them. The slaves were known as “packages” or “passengers” in the Railroad. The guides were “conductors” and the safe houses were “stations.”

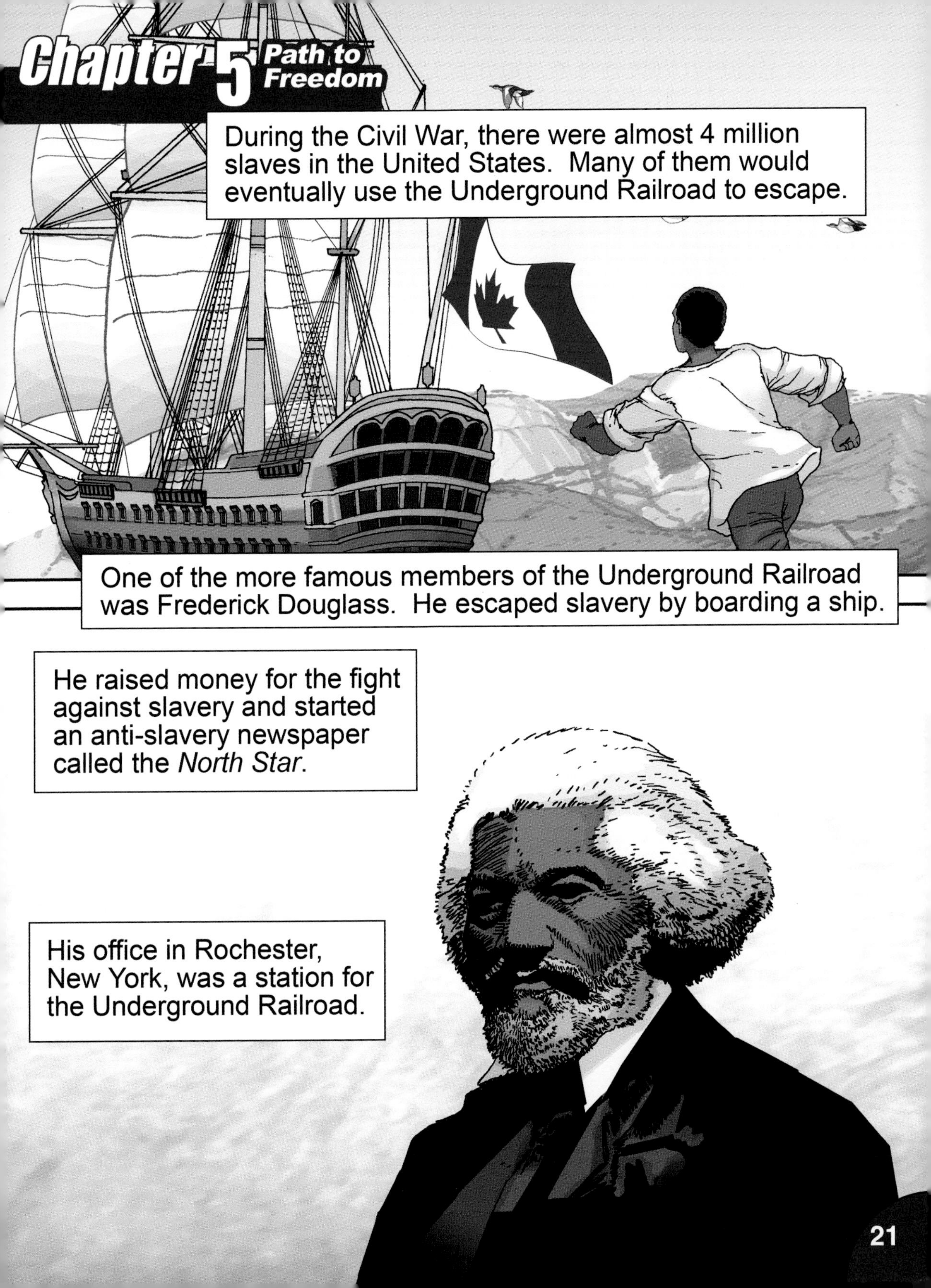
Chapter 5 Path to Freedom
During the Civil War, there were almost 4 million slaves in the United States. Many of them would eventually use the Underground Railroad to escape.
One of the more famous members of the Underground Railroad was Frederick Douglass. He escaped slavery by boarding a ship.
He raised money for the fight against slavery and started an anti-slavery newspaper called the *North Star*.
His office in Rochester, New York, was a station for the Underground Railroad.

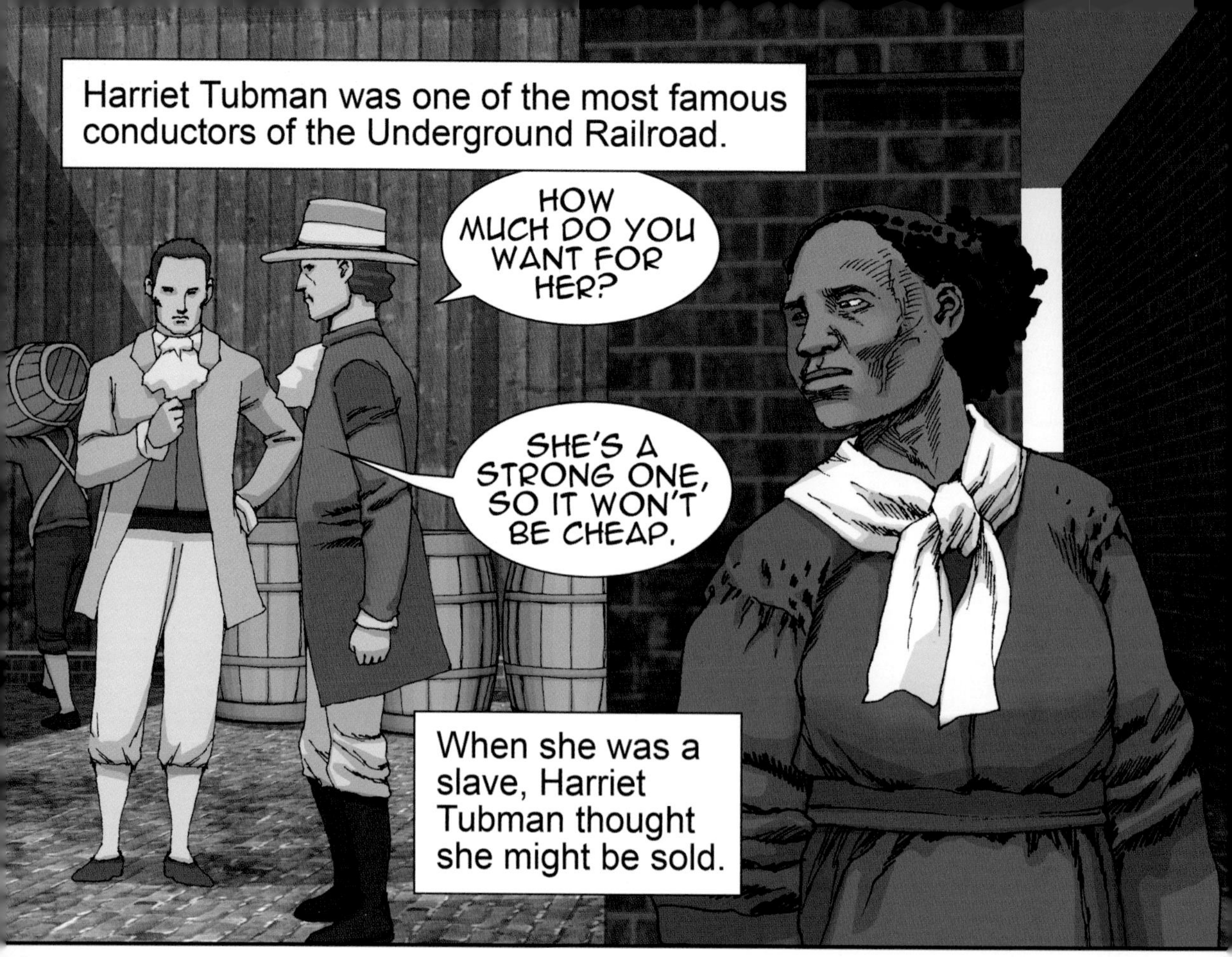
Harriet Tubman was one of the most famous conductors of the Underground Railroad.
HOW MUCH DO YOU WANT FOR HER?
SHE'S A STRONG ONE, SO IT WON'T BE CHEAP.
When she was a slave, Harriet Tubman thought she might be sold.

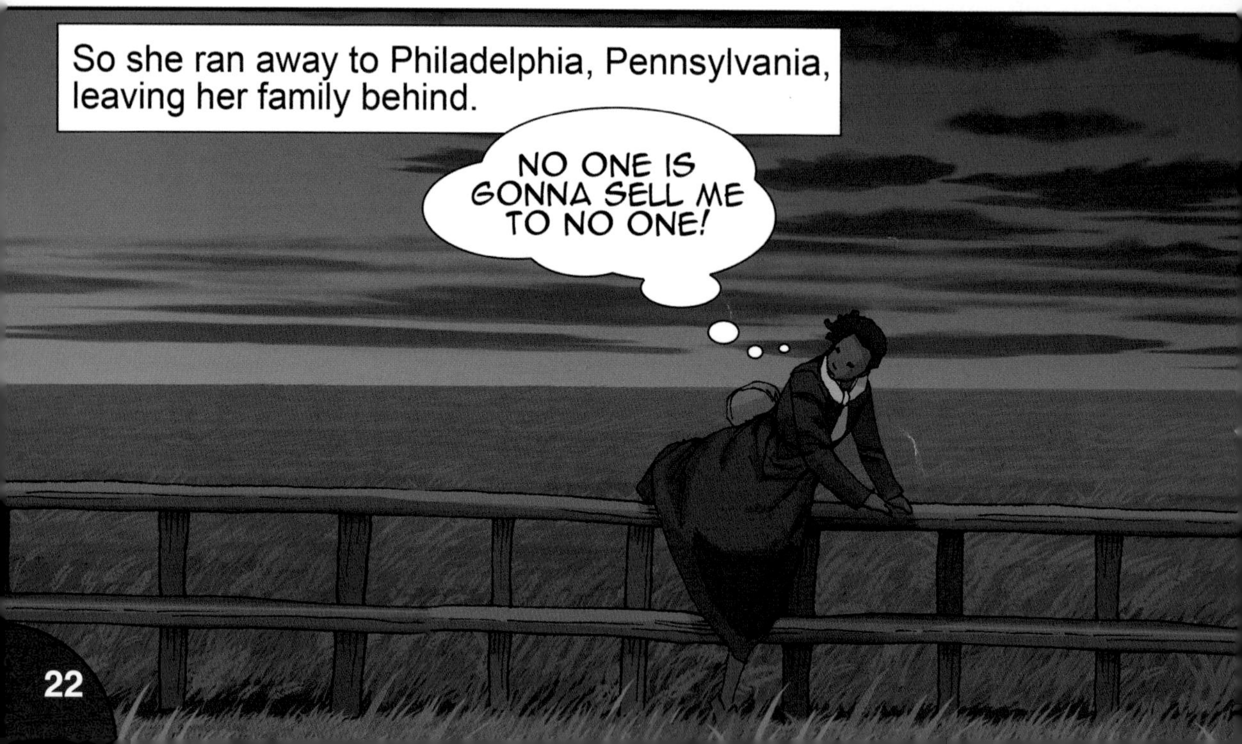
So she ran away to Philadelphia, Pennsylvania, leaving her family behind.
NO ONE IS GONNA SELL ME TO NO ONE!

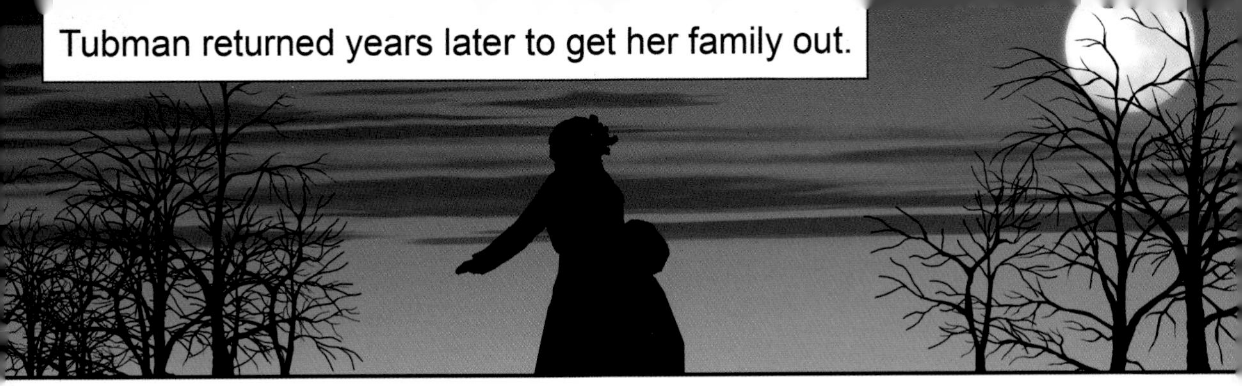
Tubman returned years later to get her family out.

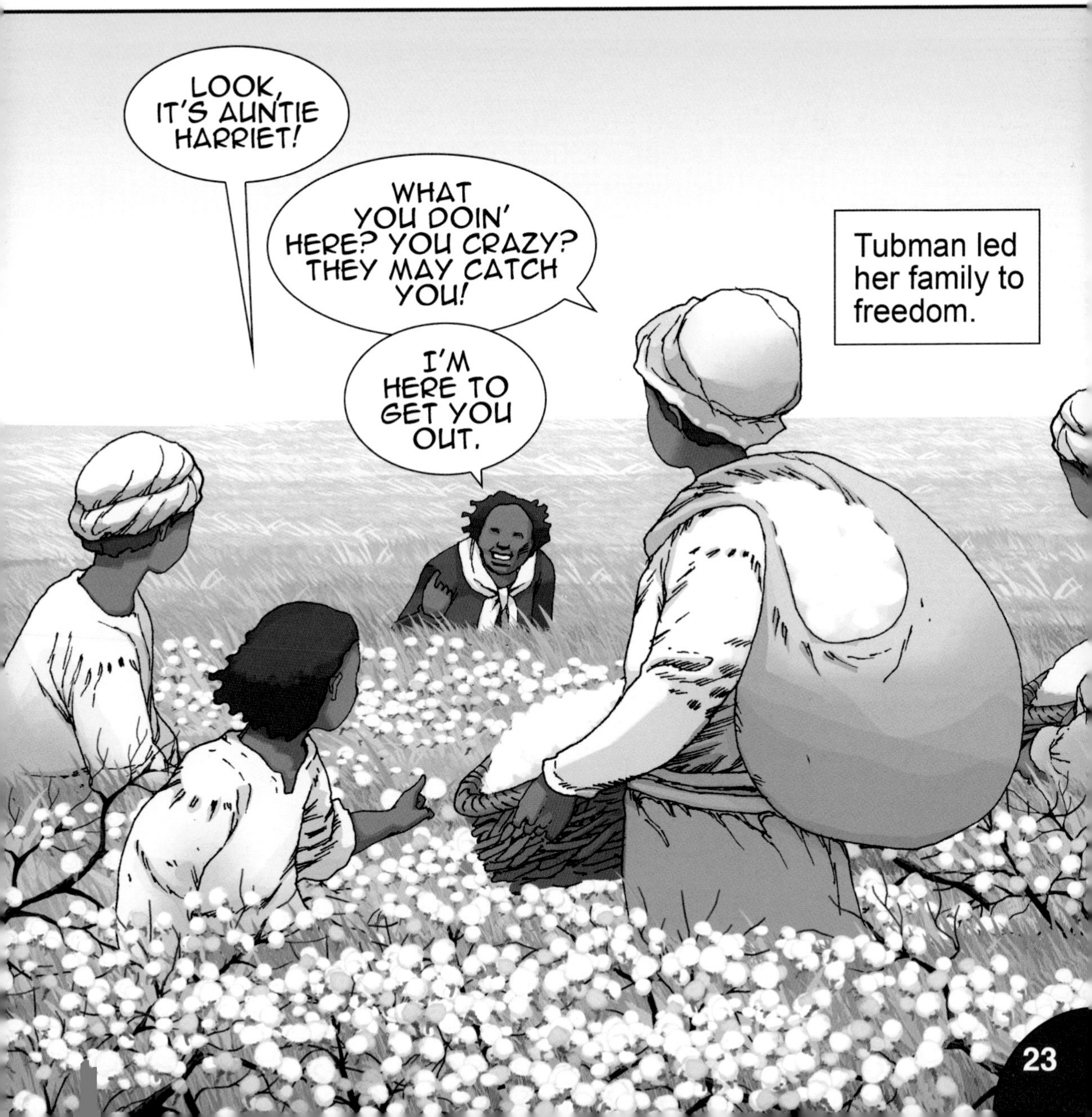
LOOK, IT'S AUNTIE HARRIET!
WHAT YOU DOIN' HERE? YOU CRAZY? THEY MAY CATCH YOU!
I'M HERE TO GET YOU OUT.
Tubman led her family to freedom.

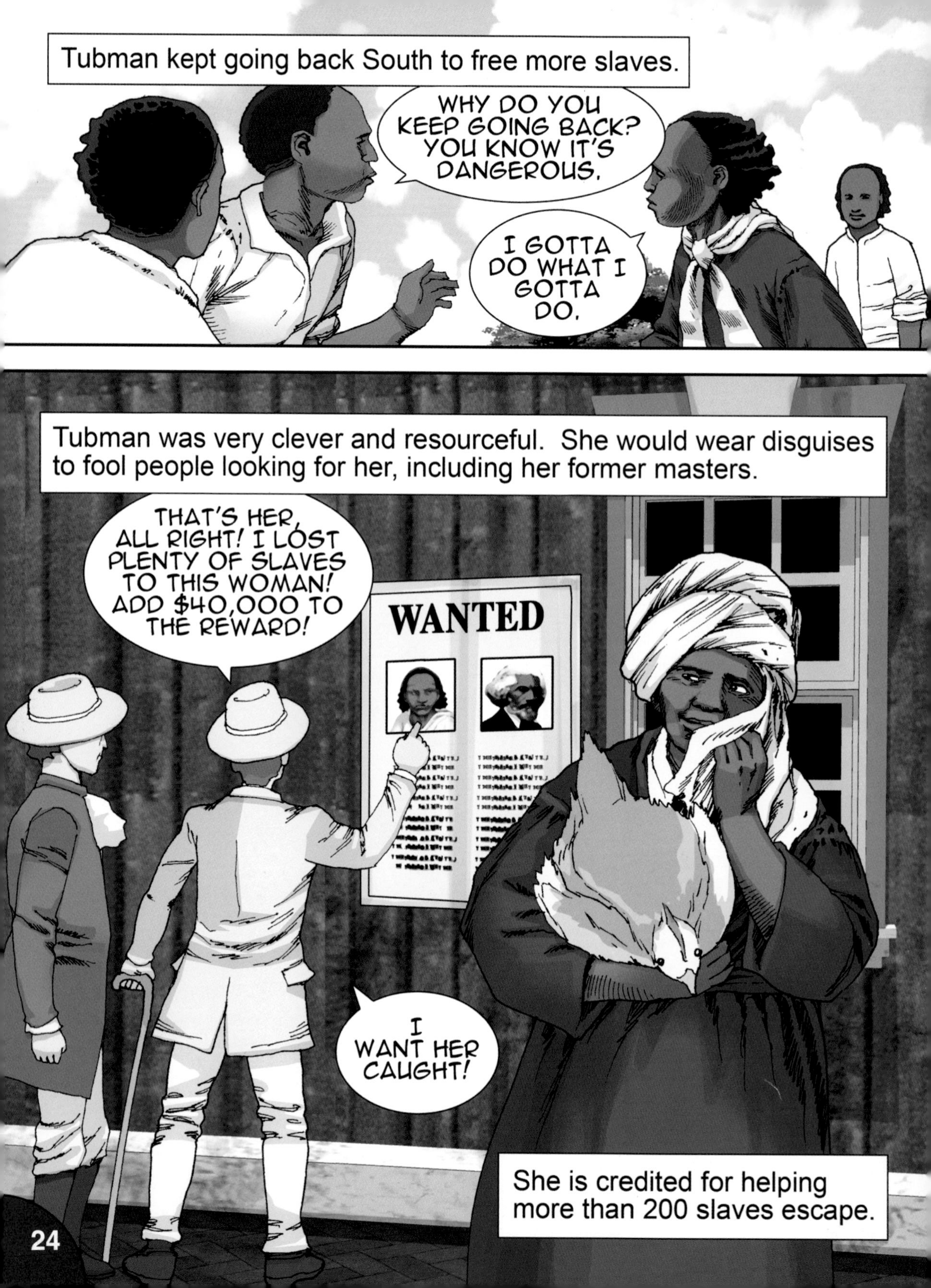
Tubman kept going back South to free more slaves.
WHY DO YOU KEEP GOING BACK? YOU KNOW IT'S DANGEROUS.
I GOTTA DO WHAT I GOTTA DO.
Tubman was very clever and resourceful. She would wear disguises to fool people looking for her, including her former masters.
THAT'S HER, ALL RIGHT! I LÓST PLENTY OF SLAVES TO THIS WOMAN! ADD $40,000 TO THE REWARD!
WANTED
I WANT HER CAUGHT!
She is credited for helping more than 200 slaves escape.

Chapter 6 The End of African Slavery

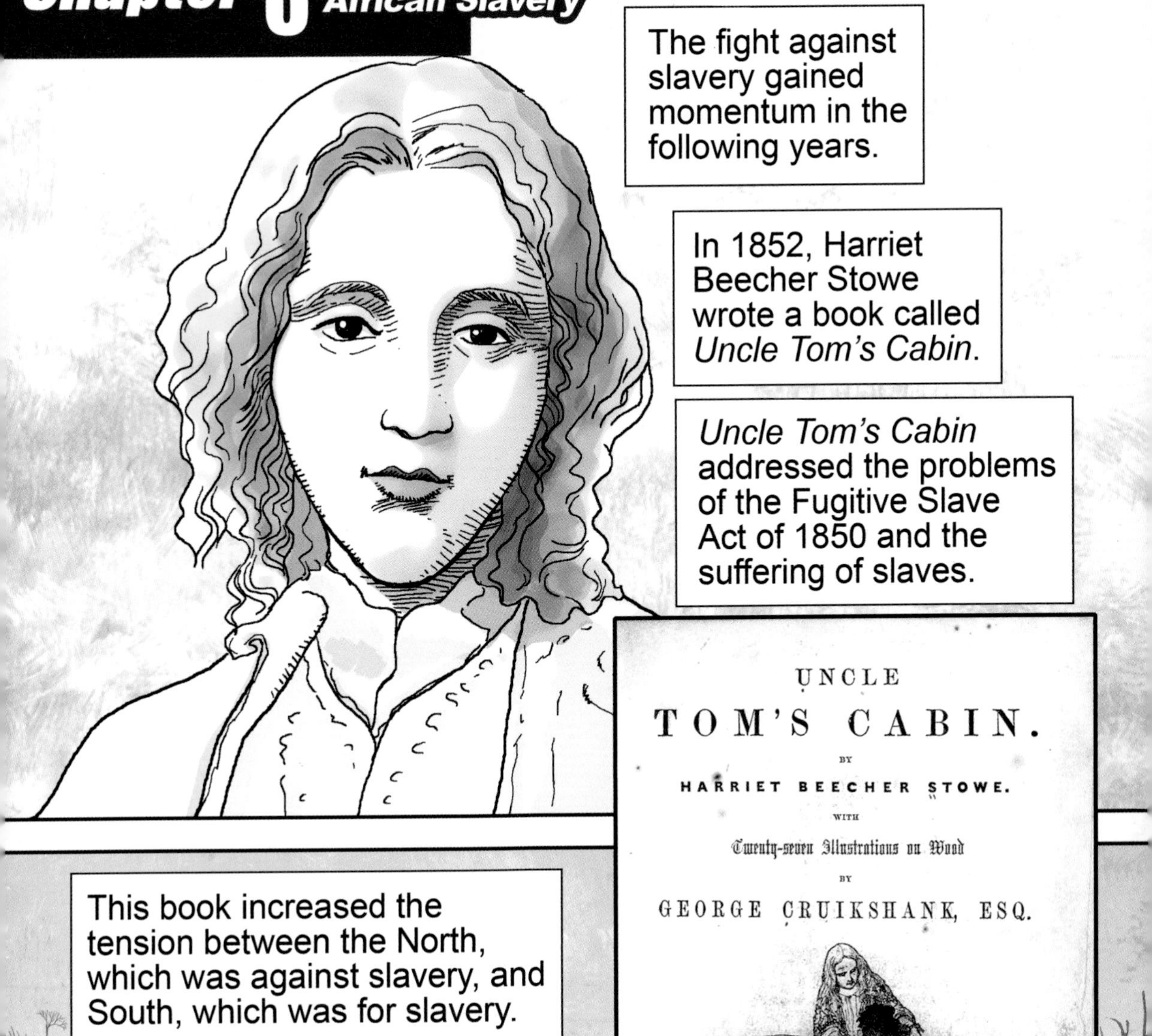
The fight against slavery gained momentum in the following years.
In 1852, Harriet Beecher Stowe wrote a book called *Uncle Tom's Cabin*.
Uncle Tom's Cabin addressed the problems of the Fugitive Slave Act of 1850 and the suffering of slaves.

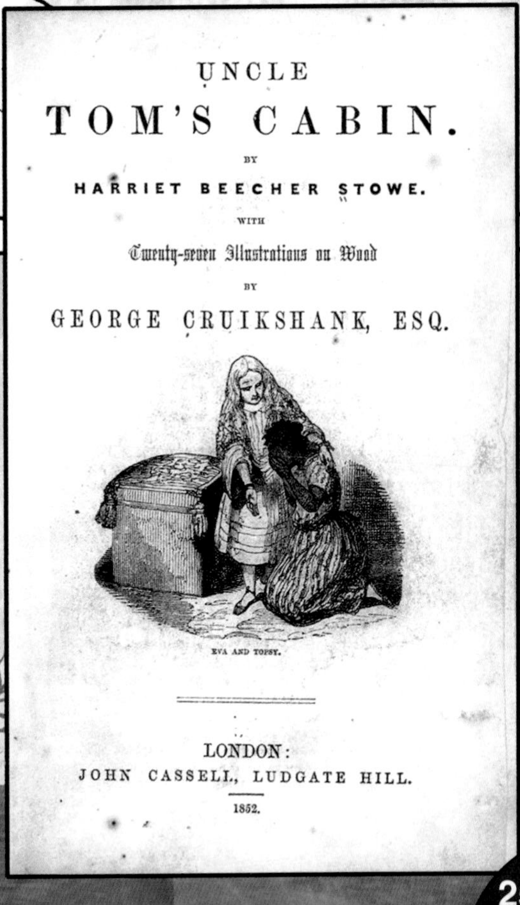

UNCLE

TOM'S CABIN.

BY

HARRIET BEECHER STOWE.

WITH

Twenty-seven Illustrations on Wood

BY

GEORGE CRUIKSHANK, ESQ.

EVA AND TOPSY.

LONDON:

JOHN CASSELL, LUDGATE HILL.

1852.

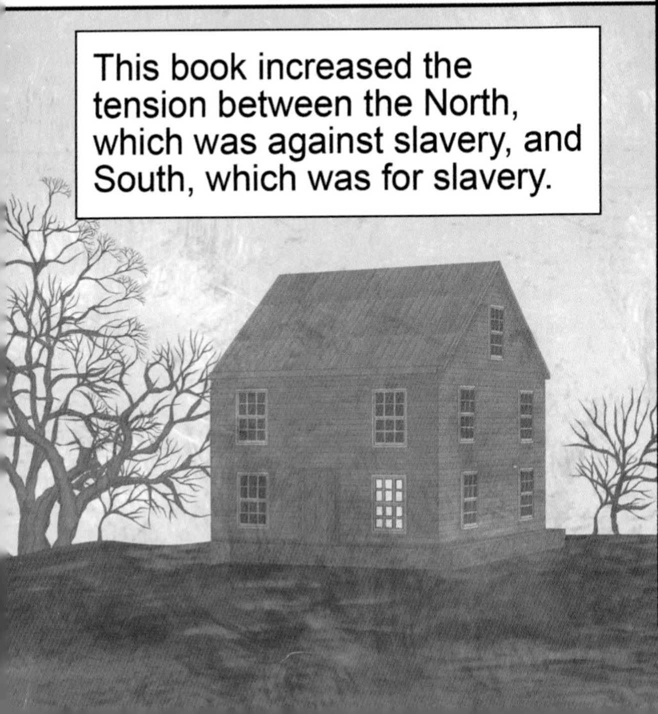
This book increased the tension between the North, which was against slavery, and South, which was for slavery.

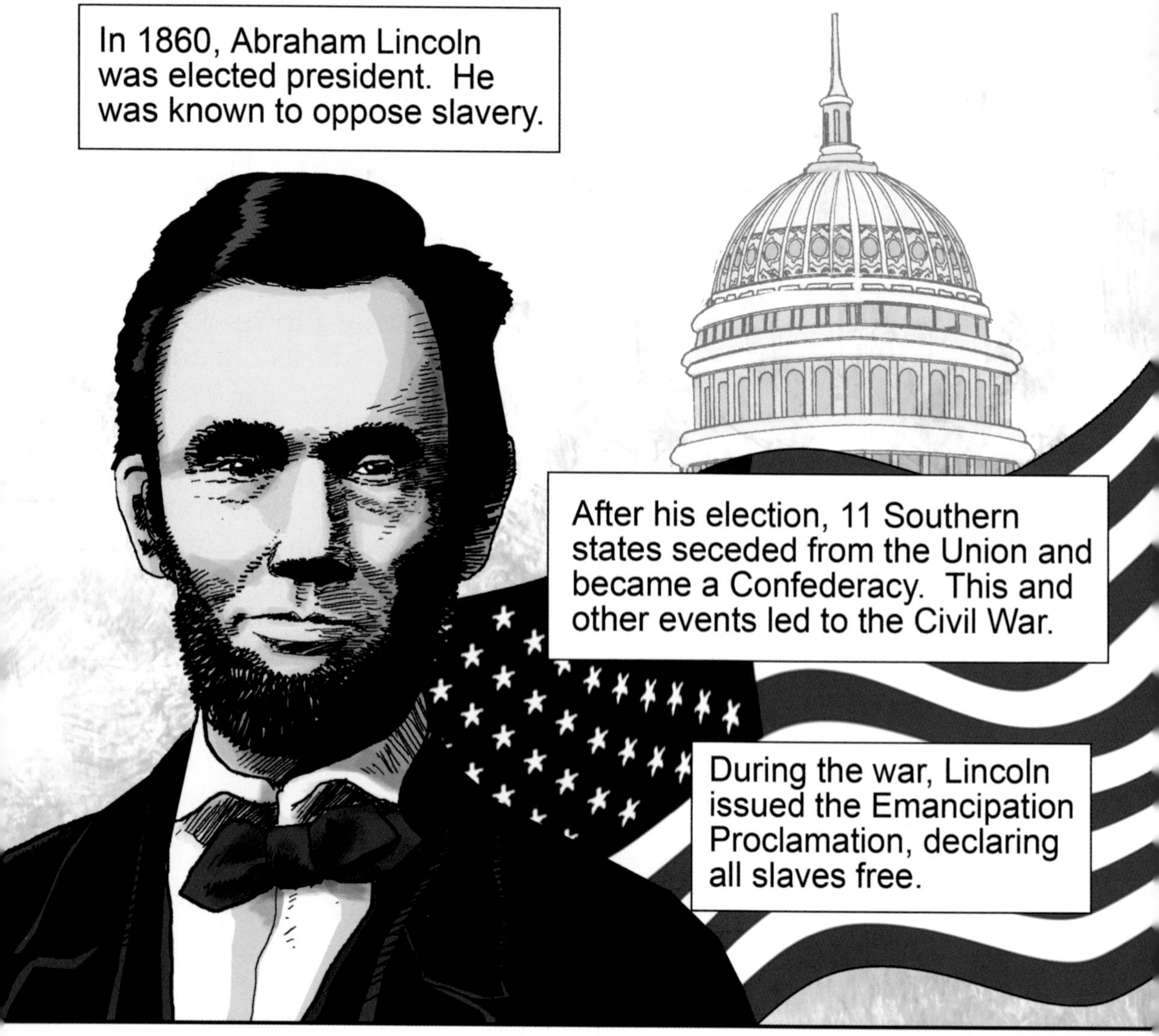
In 1860, Abraham Lincoln was elected president. He was known to oppose slavery.
After his election, 11 Southern states seceded from the Union and became a Confederacy. This and other events led to the Civil War.
During the war, Lincoln issued the Emancipation Proclamation, declaring all slaves free.

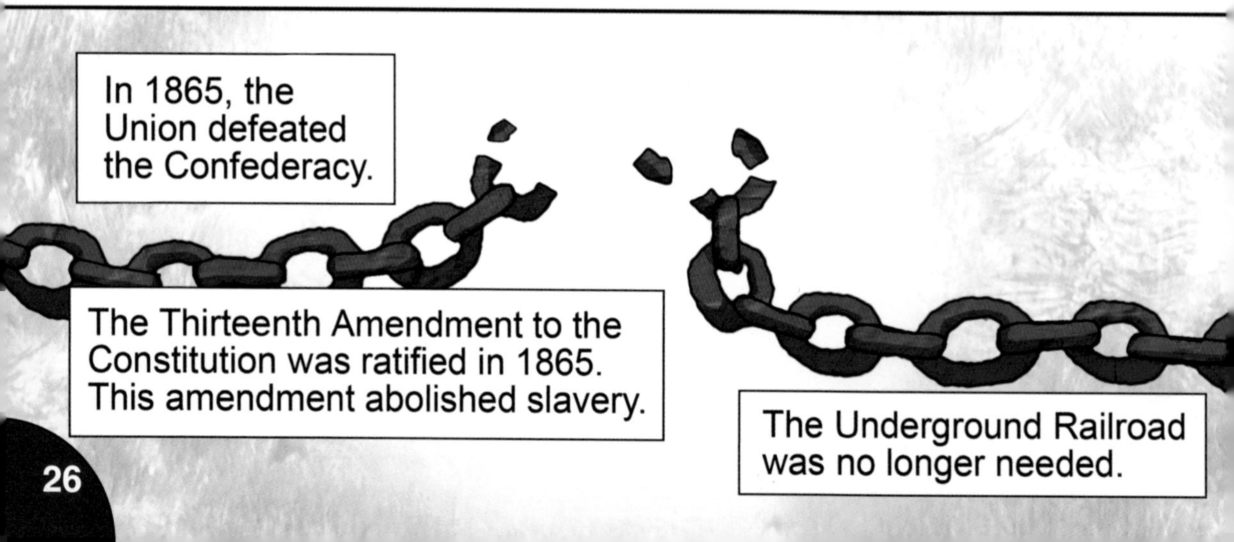
In 1865, the Union defeated the Confederacy.
The Thirteenth Amendment to the Constitution was ratified in 1865. This amendment abolished slavery.
The Underground Railroad was no longer needed.

History and Laws of the United States Regarding Slavery

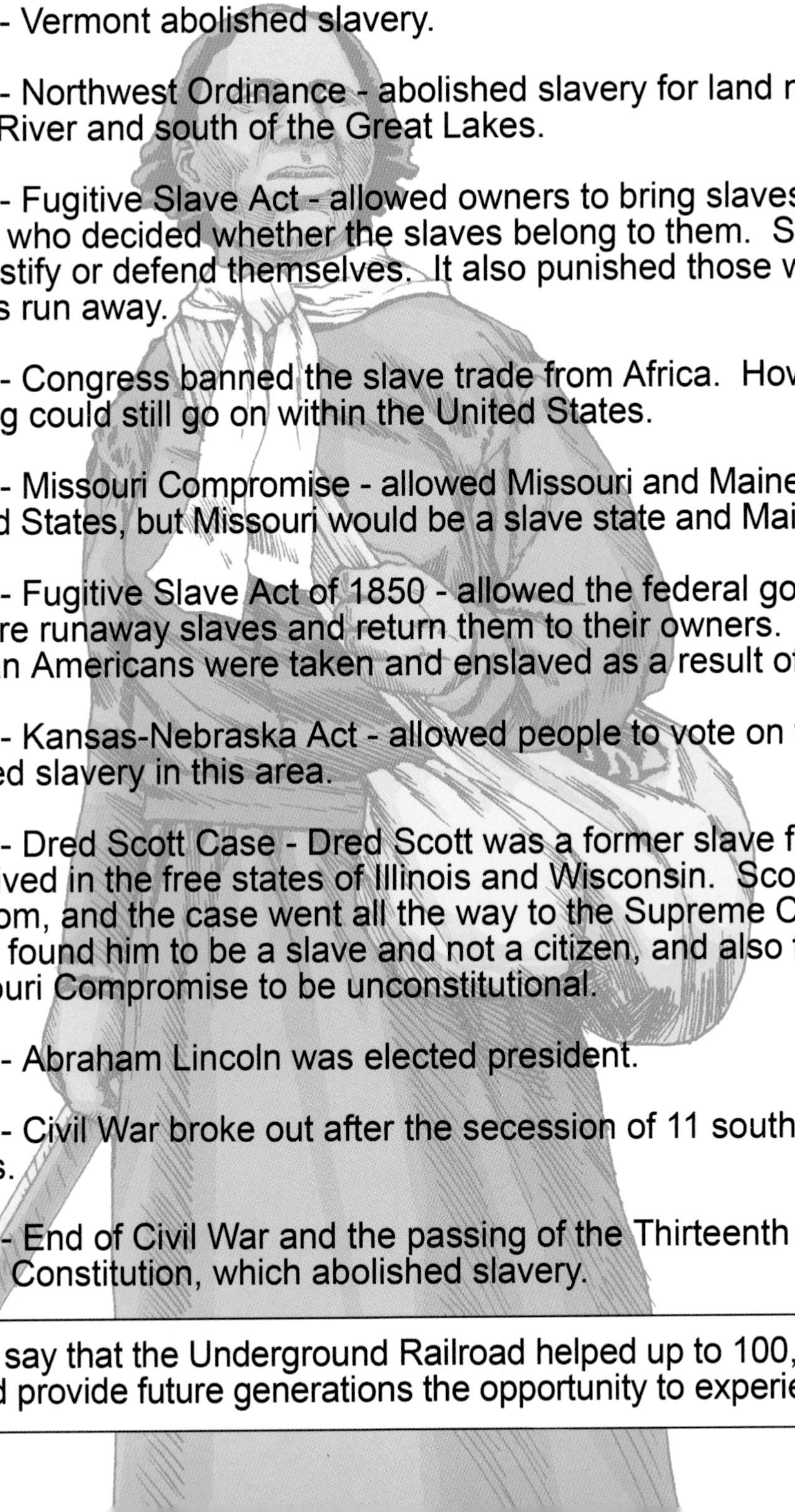

1777 - Vermont abolished slavery.

1787 - Northwest Ordinance - abolished slavery for land north of the Ohio River and south of the Great Lakes.

1793 - Fugitive Slave Act - allowed owners to bring slaves before a judge who decided whether the slaves belong to them. Slaves could not testify or defend themselves. It also punished those who helped slaves run away.

1808 - Congress banned the slave trade from Africa. However, slave trading could still go on within the United States.

1820 - Missouri Compromise - allowed Missouri and Maine to join the United States, but Missouri would be a slave state and Maine would not.

1850 - Fugitive Slave Act of 1850 - allowed the federal government to capture runaway slaves and return them to their owners. Many free African Americans were taken and enslaved as a result of this law.

1854 - Kansas-Nebraska Act - allowed people to vote on whether they wanted slavery in this area.

1857 - Dred Scott Case - Dred Scott was a former slave from Missouri who lived in the free states of Illinois and Wisconsin. Scott sued for his freedom, and the case went all the way to the Supreme Court. The Court found him to be a slave and not a citizen, and also found the Missouri Compromise to be unconstitutional.

1860 - Abraham Lincoln was elected president.

1861 - Civil War broke out after the secession of 11 southern slave states.

1865 - End of Civil War and the passing of the Thirteenth Amendment to the Constitution, which abolished slavery.

Some say that the Underground Railroad helped up to 100,000 slaves. It helped provide future generations the opportunity to experience freedom.

Map of Civil War Slave & Free States

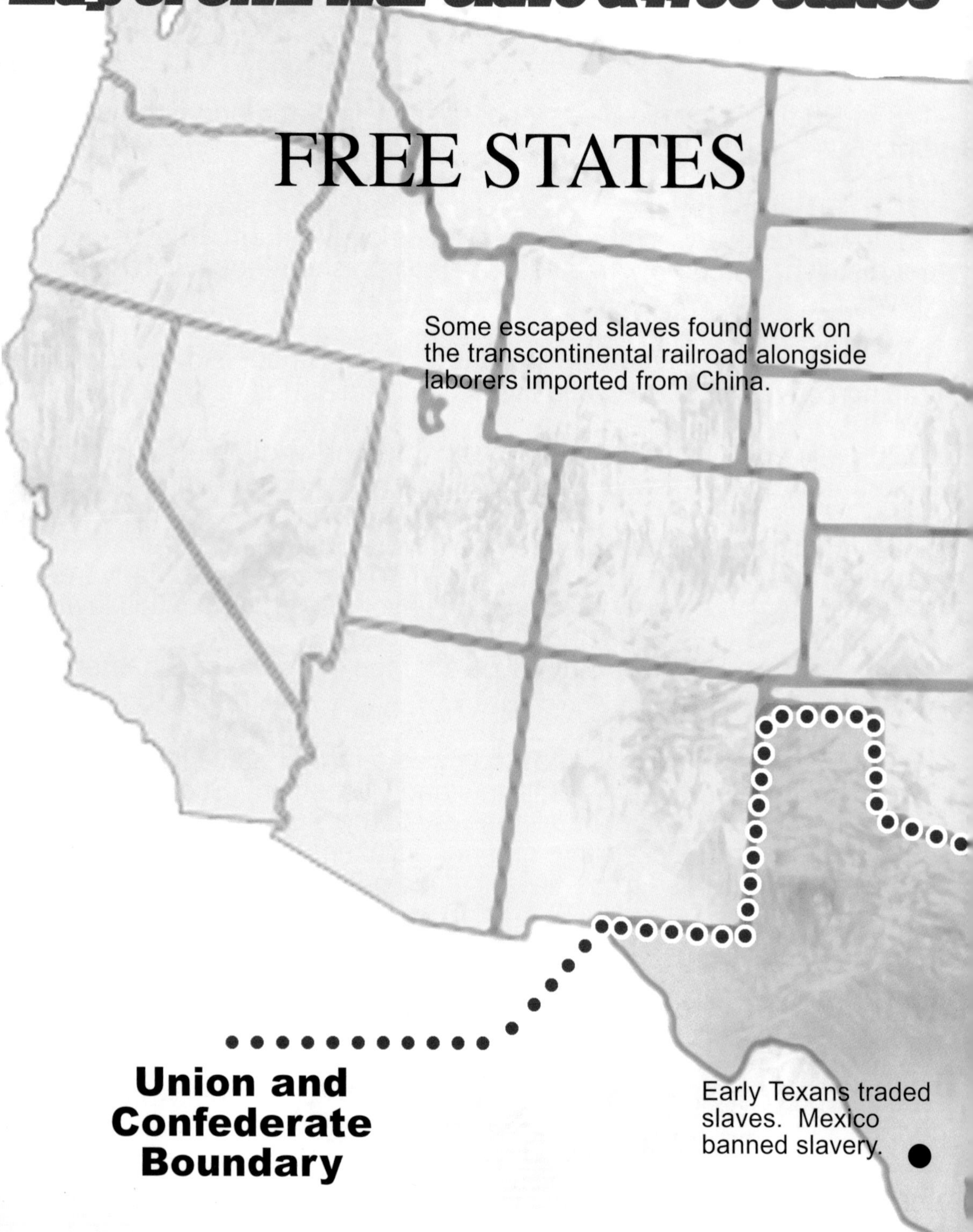
FREE STATES
Some escaped slaves found work on the transcontinental railroad alongside laborers imported from China.
Union and Confederate Boundary
Early Texans traded slaves. Mexico banned slavery.

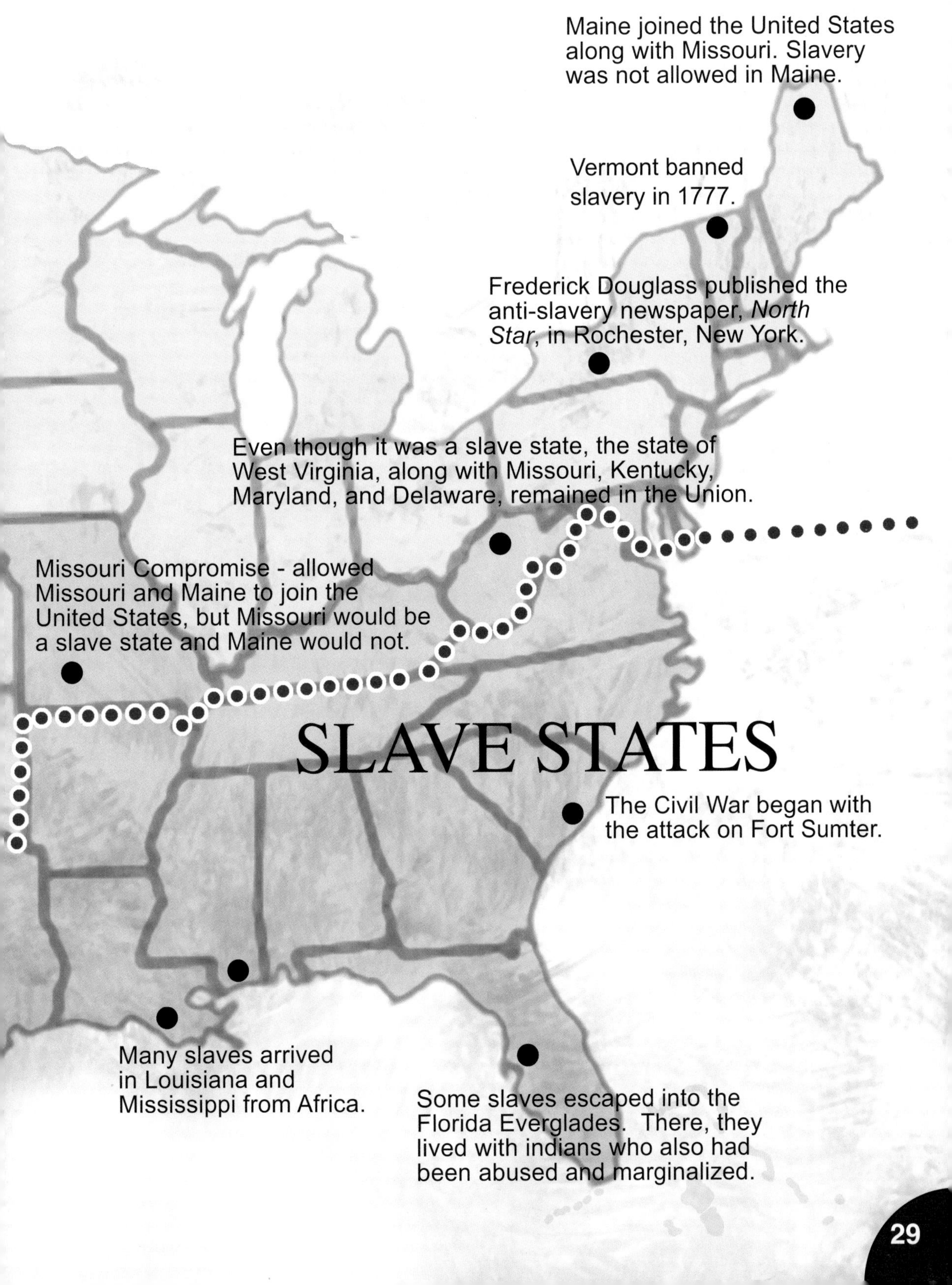
Maine joined the United States along with Missouri. Slavery was not allowed in Maine.
Vermont banned slavery in 1777.
Frederick Douglass published the anti-slavery newspaper, *North Star*, in Rochester, New York.
Even though it was a slave state, the state of West Virginia, along with Missouri, Kentucky, Maryland, and Delaware, remained in the Union.
Missouri Compromise - allowed Missouri and Maine to join the United States, but Missouri would be a slave state and Maine would not.
SLAVE STATES
The Civil War began with the attack on Fort Sumter.
Many slaves arrived in Louisiana and Mississippi from Africa.
Some slaves escaped into the Florida Everglades. There, they lived with indians who also had been abused and marginalized.

Timeline

1790s - Isaac Hopper helped fugitive slaves.

1820s - Levi Coffin began a route from North Carolina to Indiana.

1831 - William Lloyd Garrison began an anti-slavery newspaper.

1833 - The American Anti-Slavery Society began.

1844 - Codes for the Underground Railroad began using words used in railroading.

1847 - William Still opened a package to find it contained an escaped Henry Brown.

1850 - Congress passed the Fugitive Slave Act. Harriet Tubman became a conductor after her escape.

1861 - The Civil War began.

1865 - The 13th Amendment freed African Americans.

Glossary

abolitionist - someone who is against slavery.

civil war - a war between groups in the same country. The United States of America and the Confederate States of America fought a civil war from 1861 to 1865.

raid - a sudden attack.

ratify - to officially approve.

rebellion - an armed resistance or defiance of a government.

secede - to break away from a group.

Web Sites

To learn more about the Underground Railroad, visit ABDO Publishing Company on the World Wide Web at **www.abdopublishing.com**. Web sites about the Underground Railroad are featured on our Book Links page. These links are routinely monitored and updated to provide the most current information available.

Index